*Bede Griffiths: Friend and Gift of the Spirit*

Father Bede walks from breakfast to his hut

# Bede Griffiths:
*Friend and Gift of the Spirit*

by
Meath Conlan, Ph.D.

Templegate Publishers
Springfield, Illinois

First published in 2006 by
Templegate Publishers, LLC
302 East Adams Street
P.O. Box 5152
Springfield, Illinois 62705-5152
217-522-3353
templegate.com

Copyright © 2006 Meath Conlan
ISBN 10: 0-87243-270-X
ISBN 13: 978-0-87243-270-3
Library of Congress Control Number
2006907987

Without limiting the rights under copyright reserved above,
no part of this publication may be reproduced, stored in or introduced
into a retrieval system, or transmitted, in any form, or by any means
(electronic, mechanical, photocopying, recording, or otherwise),
without the prior written permission of the above
publisher of this book

To my mother Nancy, for her hard work, persistence,
and for showing me the beauty of the English language;
For my father Doug, who always told wonderful stories of his life;
and
Adrian Walsh, who is kind, knowledgeable and wise.

# Contents

| | |
|---|---|
| Introduction | 9 |
| Foreword | 15 |
| Prologue | 17 |
| 1: Developing a Contemplative Approach to Life | 21 |
| 2: Love is the Golden String | 27 |
| 3: Meditation as a Way of Self-transcendence | 33 |
| 4. The Practice of the Presence of God | 43 |
| 5: The Indian Stages of Life | 53 |
| 6. Finding Spirituality in the Ordinary | 59 |
| 7: Contemplation as a Whole Way of Life | 65 |
| 8: A New Way of Life – Living from the Centre | 71 |
| 9: Expressing the Inexpressible – The Six Vajra Verses | 79 |
| 10: Inter-spiritual Dialogue – A Journey of Surrender | 85 |
| 11: Two Elders Meet Across the Traditions | 91 |
| 12: Appreciating the Greatness in Others | 99 |
| 13: God and the Universe are not Two | 103 |
| 14: Meditation – Some Practical Guidance | 111 |
| Postscript | 119 |
| Glossary | 121 |
| Select Bibliography | 123 |
| Index | 125 |
| About the Author | 127 |

# Introduction

Bede Griffiths is considered by many to be one of the greatest mystics of modern times. He was my mentor and friend for many years and had a profound influence on my approach to spirituality. He was born Alan Richard Griffiths in 1906 at Walton-on-Thames, England. Experiencing a conversion to Catholicism in his late twenties (1931), he became a Benedictine monk a year later, at which time he was given the name "Bede."

Over the next twenty years, Bede Griffiths led a traditional monastic life, initially in England but later heading a monastery in France and then another in Scotland. By the mid-1950s, however, he realized that the traditional Western focus on the rational, the masculine, and the patriarchal was no longer serving the deeper aspirations of spiritual seekers.

Inspired by his studies into Eastern thought and at the invitation of another Benedictine who wished to establish Benedictine Monasticism in India, Bede transferred to the Kurisumala Ashram in Kerala, where he adopted the Sanskrit name, "Dhayananda." Here he developed for himself, and nurtured in others, the discovery of the feminine side of God, the intuitive, imaginative, artistic and poetic aspects of the human mind and heart. For many visitors to India, he was able, through his talks, to soften the hard edges of dogma and doctrine with an understanding of Eastern and Western mysticism. In fact, Fr. Bede's vision was to renew the contemplative life through the "marriage of East and West" and of science and mysticism. He had a keen interest and involvement in East-West inter-religious dialogue, which flowed from his conviction that, while religions on a superficial level are all naturally quite different and separate, the deeper one researches the spirit of all religions the more they converge on a common centre.

Initially through correspondence, I met Fr. Bede in 1976-77, and studied and lived with him in India for a number of years. He was my mentor, but also my friend, and the person who most inspired my spiritual counseling practice. Bede was ultimately concerned with the "search for God," the continual effort to "realize" God, to discover the reality of the hidden presence of God in the cave of the heart or depths of the soul. It was this above all that he wished to share respectfully with me and with all who came to the ashram. He had a listening heart that was finely attuned to others. Those who left his presence frequently remarked that he treated them as if they were his only business that day.

It is a difficult and rare virtue to mean what we say, to love without deceit, to think no evil, to bear no grudge, to be free from selfishness, to be innocent, straightforward and simple-hearted. Yet this was Bede; a monk with a universal heart, an icon of integrity and guilelessness.

In 1984 my decision to journey to India for sabbatical leave was a milestone in achieving spiritual balance in my daily life: leaving behind excessive activity and developing more seriously the contemplative arts. In my twenties much of what I did was in terms of measurable results. I needed to find the middle way. In a private letter of 1977 Bede advised me: "leave the results of your work to God . . . then you will not be disturbed . . . and keep evenness of mind in contemplation."

Bede Griffiths saw that humanity is entering upon a new age. The dominance of Western culture was, he maintained, coming to an end with the future belonging to Asia, Latin America and Africa. While not at all rejecting his Western heritage — for it has much to commend it — he felt that the limitations of Western science and democracy, as derived from the Greeks, have become more apparent. He regarded the artistic, cultural, architectural, and philosophical achievements of Western culture as crucial to the balance and harmony in which civilized life could develop. But at the Renaissance, this harmony, he declared, was lost, and the dominant, aggressive, competitive rational mind of Western man took over. Bede called for a restoration of balance in a meeting between East and West, at the deepest level of consciousness. He suggested that the problem of imbalance is also a matter of importance for religion. In the West religion has been shaped by building structures of doctrine, discipline, law and morality; and Western science, with its attachment to observation and experiment, remains firmly in this mode of Greek and scholastic thought.

Bede Griffiths had 'his finger on the pulse' of modern life. He said, in regard to the hundreds of visitors travelling from all over the world to the *ashram* in search for meaning and purpose in their lives: "Today it is not through the externals of religion, whether in doctrine or in discipline, that most people are finding God, but in the experience of the indwelling Spirit, the presence of God in the heart."

In the late 1970s, Professor Colin Williams stated that Australia was the most secular country in the world. Author and academic Manning Clark posited a similar view. He said that in writing his history of Australia, he wanted to tell the story of a country that had decided to live without God. Yet, in spite of the persistence of this myth, there seems to be an understanding of and interest in spirituality and moments of transcendence. Broadcaster Caroline Jones noted in her book from the popular national ABC television series, *The Search for Meaning*: "Even in the most oppressive circumstances there seems to be choices which open up meaning and presence which is larger than the limited perspectives on life that [are] present[ed] as total."

American author Thomas Moore asserts that spirituality germinates in the mundane and finds its nurturing in the "smallest of daily activities." He says that spirituality is an effective source of healing for psychological wounds yet is hidden under the guise of ordinariness. It is a widespread perception that traditional religion has often failed to meet contemporary spiritual needs. People everywhere are on a quest for a life of depth, meaning and self-transcendence. For at least three decades I have been aware of people moving towards alternative spiritual paths, nurturing their inner lives by self-discovery. From what I experienced of Bede Griffiths' characteristic style with people, every seeker who visited Shantivanam was treated with respect for their individual journey, with kindness for anyone who suffered, and with genuine friendship for all.

The idea of writing this book arose with my wish to reflect on my seventeen year friendship with the late Bede Griffiths and to share with others the significance and meaning of what I had found. I selected a number of incidents, or vignettes, which are arranged as memoir. All those chosen are factual, gathered from my various notebooks, journals, and correspondence; the events did occur and are presented as a truthful version of what I remember.

The search for meaning and self-transcendence is a significant human experience that requires description. It is my hope that the following memoir vignettes will provide sources of reflection for people who find themselves at spiritual crossroads. I hope those who knew Father Bede will enjoy revisiting their friend through the following incidents. Finally, I trust this book will be an encouragement for seekers, who, without having met him personally, have been inspired by his life and thought.

I offer my thanks to Thomas Garvey, the owner of Templegate Publishers who first contacted me with his invitation to write a col-

*Introduction*

lection of stories for his company. He has remained a patient and enthusiastic adviser, and a real pleasure to work with. My thanks and esteem also go to John Wilkins, editor for many years of *The Tablet* in London who graciously believed in my ability as a writer, and accepted my work for *The Tablet*. I am indebted for their firm friendship to members of the Bede Griffiths Trust, Sister Pascaline Coff, OSB, John Douglas and Brother John Martin. Thanks to Australian documentary filmmaker Nicholas Partridge with whom I enjoy vigorous conversations and to Canon Frank Sheehan of Christchurch Ethics Centre. To my friend Anne Day who urges me to write. For first introducing me to the writings of Bede Griffiths I am indebted to Christine and Bill Brennan of Denmark. For his uncompromising loyalty and fond friendship, I wish to express my gratitude to Adrian Walsh, MD, of New York. His breadth of knowledge, common sense and compassion are a beacon for me. Kerrie Reid, Alan Croker and Andrew Howie are three friends in Sydney whose hospitality has been invaluable. For his exemplary witness to interfaith dialogue, and for his valued friendship, I am indebted to the Tibetan Buddhist teacher, His Eminence Khejok Tulku Rinpoche. The Bott family of Perth extended hospitality and encouragement to me over many years. I extend thanks also to my friends in the academy; Dr Peter Willis and Dr Loretta do Rosario. For giving me a friendly space in which to write, I thank Dr Anthony Kain in Adelaide. For their open door, I thank Gianni and Eleonora Armani of Rome. Robert Carey for his courage, Barry Dwyer, David Roach, Michael Mifsud for their loyalty. Laurence Freeman, and Emilie and the late Dr Sipphanonda Ketudat. Thanks to Herb Elliott, with whom I climbed the Himalayas and rafted down the Ganges, and who provides me with inspiration in combining spirituality with common sense. Also Mark and Cate Hohnen, who believed in my work. Jan and Barry Walsh, and their large family, with whom I enjoyed many 'curry nights' on their farm, not far from the No. 1 Rabbit Proof Fence. John Sumich, a man of courage and generosity, and my loyal friends George and Dr Anthea Kingsley. Del and Dan Duffy, whose door was always open. John T. Walsh, my kind host in New York. Ken Holland, Rick and Jacinta Rimmington. Roland Ropers and Christiane May-Ropers, my wonderful and creative friends in Munich. Bruce Gates and Kieran McAlinden, for their constant friendship. Rhonda and Michael Perrott who for years supported my work. Maria Fede Caproni and Pietro Armani, dear friends in Rome. Helen Bunning, David Bott, Jack Baker, Jann McPherson, and Mandy and Stephen Skipper for hours of fruitful conversation. From California I thank Barry and Kipra Heerman for their friendly encouragement and hospitality, Dianne Edleman who is generous, talented and savvy, and Cherie and Dan Porter who have been strong in their friendship. In New York I also count among my many kind friends Val and Joan Taubner, Phil and Mary Schwab, John and Helen Lautner and Marilyn and Jerry Gagnon. Fr Carl Arico and Father Thomas Keating, OCSO, of Contemplative Outreach have been terrific spiritual mentors. For the example of interfaith courage I thank Abbot Placid Spearritt, OSB, of The Benedictine Abbey, New Norcia. Throughout his 1992 Australian tour Father Bede was cared for by the kind Sisters of Saint John of God and the Sisters of Saint Joseph in Perth, the Good Samaritan Sisters in Melbourne, the Cistercian Monks in rural Victoria, the Marist Fathers in Sydney. I offer profound thanks to these communities. For her friendship and encouragement, and her kindness to Father Bede in 1992 I especially thank Joan Halsall. Finally I thank my mother Nancy Conlan who, at 84 years of age, read and amended the drafts of this book for clarity of expression prior to my sending the manuscript to my publishers.

Meath Conlan<br>Perth, February 2006

# Foreword

Wisdom distilled and made delectable from the heart of a prophet is truly the gift of this small volume. It enables those in search of a contemplative life to be present for the profound spiritual sharing of director and directee, of master and disciple, over many intermittent sabbaticals at *Shantivanam* in south India. Deep gratitude cannot but well up toward Meath Conlan as he tunes the reader in on these intimate spiritual sessions he so richly received from this authentic modern day mystic, Fr. Bede Griffiths. Knowing Meath's other gifted writings, many of us encouraged him to write this volume in the hope that a broader audience could share these treasures from the heart of a master describing the contemplative life. For Fr. Bede Griffiths, who had the heart of Christ, it must have delighted that heart to find one so open and eager, so hungry for the contemplative life. As he did on many other occasions, the Spirit moved Fr. Bede to invite this Aussie from "down under" to come for a time to live and experience contemplative prayer and the contemplative life through nature, a simplified liturgy and small dedicated community at *Shantivanam*. Coming from Australia, a country which labeled itself the "most secular in the world", Meath came, saw and allowed himself to be conquered by the Spirit. What a unique and sacred school of learning for his own vocation today and his share in the mission of the Church — spiritual counseling for contemplative life. Since, as Bede Griffiths insists, God's call to contemplation is universal, everyone should find practical and profound guidance in these pages.

Sister M. Pascaline Coff, O.S.B. O+M

# Prologue

*"Each individual person, body and soul, has a unique character, is a unique image of God, and that person will not dissolve. The more universal you become, the more deeply personal you become. You do not diffuse yourself, you do not lose yourself as you grow in knowledge and understanding and love – you extend. You do not cease to be a person. You become more deeply personal."*

Bede Griffiths, The Cosmic Revelation, p. 127

Father Bede Griffiths' second journey to Australia in 1992 was a gruelling test of his commitment "to spread the word." But what was the 'word' he wished to spread, and at such cost to his health? It was simply this – an extension of his vision to renew the contemplative life for contemporary humankind. Yes there were many issues that he liked to speak about and with which he kept up-to-date through the news media. Included among these were issues of liturgical reform, international politics and economics, the environment, the state of the poor in the Third World, interfaith dialogue, and the interface of science and mysticism. But he always advocated this basic teaching of contemplative renewal and the primacy of transcendent love.

After his first stroke he said to my mother and father and me: "I have learnt more in the last two years of my life than in all of my life before the stroke." He avowed that during the period of his stroke and the time of convalescence he felt as if he "was being overwhelmed by love." This perhaps is the reason why he felt he had "to make good use of the remaining time left to me, to travel and share what I have discovered with as many people as I can."

He realized that popularity and superficial teachings could lead people into more confusion than into the light. Wary as he was of seeking popularity, he would step back and detach himself from the results of his speaking engagements. Though he took his message seriously, himself he never did. The priority in all his lectures and interviews was to communicate not so much a sense of learned exposition, but of the presence of God. Bede related an amusing story about a scholar who was delivering a lecture on the *Bhagavad Gita* in Sanskrit. In time the audience became bored and one by one nearly everyone left. Finally only one old man was left sitting enraptured before him. The lecturer, naturally feeling appreciated by the old man went up to him at the close of the evening and said: "I'm glad to know you appreciated my talk." "I wasn't listening to your talk at

Father Bede "at the controls" of Paul Terry's Citation for the flight from Perth to Albany

all," was the reply. So the lecturer said, "But you were showing such rapt attention." "Ah!" said the old man, "but I saw Krishna in front of you and I was worshipping Krishna. I wasn't listening to your talk."

Having delivered two major lectures in Perth before more than 5000 people, and having shared in the ceremonies to welcome His Holiness the Dalai Lama before 20,000 people, Bede was happy to accept Joan and Paul Terry's hospitality to rest at "*Maitraya*," their farm overlooking the Southern Ocean near Albany. Together with my parents, Father Bede and I boarded Paul's Cessna Citation with Bede wearing impressive head-gear sitting by Paul at the controls. We had a wonderful few days of complete rest at the farm. I recall our host asking Father Bede: "Do you believe that there is a real and loving presence waiting to welcome you at the other side when you die?" Bede calmly nodded his head and realising the import of the question simply said,

> Yes, I do. I really do. I think this body and soul or *psyche* with all its thoughts and feelings will disintegrate in the grave. But beyond these is the *pneuma*, the Spirit. It is this that is eternal and it is my point of communion with God. I think if I have lived my life wisely, at the moment of death I can free myself of the body and soul and enter into the Spirit and union with God. That is my goal and the way I live my life.

One special day it seemed that great receptacles in the sky poured dazzling light to flood the coastline, beaches and ocean. For a while the wind abated and Bede decided to walk down to the huge granite outcrops to sit and meditate. He was a little frail, so we accompanied him, though withdrew some distance once he had selected the rock upon which he would sit and contemplate the surroundings. I remember seeing him sitting quite alone, still wearing

**Father Bede contemplates the Southern Ocean near Albany, Western Australia**

his kavi cloth from tropical India. It seemed as though those time honoured rocks saluted another time honoured presence. The grandeur all round was in vast contrast to this simple and saintly old man. Afterwards we all realised that we had experienced identical awareness, as though at the midpoint of a sacred moment, and that God is present wherever goodness and beauty abide.

# Chapter 1

## SUMMER, AUSTRALIA, 1976-1977

# Developing a Contemplative Approach to Life

*"To discover God is not to discover an idea but to discover oneself. It is to awaken to that part of one's existence which has been hidden from sight . . . The discovery may be very painful . . . a kind of death. But it is the one thing which makes life worth living."*

Bede Griffiths, The Golden String, p. 12

Trying to piece together the various influences that opened me to spiritual life is, as Bede said, "like discovering oneself," and the Spirit's guiding presence within. I entered the church at the age of nineteen in the late 1960s initially inspired by the life of a local Moslem Imam of the Afghan community in Perth. As an adolescent, I had worked since 1963 for a quarter of each year in the immense inland desert regions of Western Australia. It was while working in the Great Victoria Desert that my spiritual sense became more attuned. Work in such climes was never easy. The heat was extraordinary, the solitude immense, the need to keep pace with men far older than I great. Thinking about spirituality and philosophy helped me through the days, weeks and months, till I returned to school. Mine was not the sort of life experience one might expect of a young Australian; though without it, I doubt I would have developed my spiritual sensibilities in the way I did.

I was still in my twenties and a few years as a priest when I was appointed pastor of an extensive, sparsely populated area of Western Australia centred at Gnowangerup, and stretching to the eastern boundaries of the Fitzgerald River National Park. It was my first rural appointment, and I keenly felt the isolation and loneliness. To that point in time, family and friends had always surrounded me. To compensate for the sense of loneliness into which I felt plunged, I embraced a multiplicity of tasks that were outwardly spiritual, though kept my attention focused, not inwardly, but outside of myself, and away from the pain I felt at the time. I experienced the gradual onset of a 'crisis of faith.' Prayer lost its savour for me, my enthusiasm waned, and daily tasks became a drudge. The way ahead seemed enveloped in darkness. I felt alone and lost.

In the midst of this passage, friends sent me a small book titled *Return to the Centre*. I read it and I discovered the spirituality of Bede Griffiths, a Benedictine monk from England who had journeyed to India on a search, as he explained, "for the other half of [his] soul." His book enabled me to look for and find sources of transcendence and meaning in my work. Additionally, his autobiography *The Golden String* became an anchor-hold for me at just the right time. He wrote of the advent of the spiritual life in words that rang true: "[to] see our life for a moment or . . . in its true perspective in relation to . . . the eternal order which underlies it . . . no longer isolated individuals in conflict with our surroundings; but parts of a whole, elements in a universal harmony."

I corresponded with Dom Bede, who answered my letters quickly, and seriously, on fragile blue Indian Aerogrammes which displayed Mahatma Ghandi's portrait, and declared: "Untouchability is

*Developing a Contemplative Approach to Life*

**Father Bede at his desk — Saccidananda ashram, South India**

a crime against humanity!" Every couple of weeks I would scan the horizon for the postal truck that may bring word from India. In an early letter, I expressed concerns I had with the outward expression of ministry. In the diocesan centre, I had been used to a great deal of activity and a modest degree of outward success. However, life was very different "in the bush." The system of having two priests serve this enormous area was abandoned; and in my youthful enthusiasm, I attempted to maintain as many Masses for the small scattered communities as under the old arrangement. Thus, by force of circumstances, I found it hard to settle down to 'being' rather than 'doing', and to solitude rather than a hectic social life. In the bush, numbers or activities did not measure the notion of success. I rapidly became exhausted and dispirited. Bede observed my busy, over-active style of ministry. He advised me to sever ties with and let go of my past attachment to ego driven activity. He wrote: "Break with the past. Concentrate on the new vision of life . . . leave [the past] behind." Yet he reassured me to remain calm in attitude and practice of contemplation. This, he urged, would be the appropriate way of making the most of my time in the bush. He wrote to me, calling the loss of "the contemplative dimensions not just your problem, but a problem of the Church as a whole." In another letter, he urged

**Front gate of Saccidananda ashram — built in typical South Indian style**

me to spend a contemplative year with him at *Saccidananda ashram*, something I had to wait till 1984 to accomplish. In the meantime, our regular correspondence continued, for which I shall always be grateful. Though I did not immediately go to India, Father Bede encouraged me to embrace pastoral work ". . . as a desert experience that matures your spiritual life." 'Be still and know that I am God' (Ps.46:10)." It was then at his behest, I began to systematically read the lives of the Desert Fathers and Mothers. In these 'lives' I found a number of helpful parallels with my own ministry and life-style in the Australian bush.

My years of friendship with Bede Griffiths were influential. He drew many people from all over the world that like me sought advice and guidance for the inner journey. His spiritual vision continues to challenge and lead people toward personal renewal of contemplative living. His openness to and respect for the wisdom to be found in all religions inspires me still in my work as a spiritual director.

# Chapter 2

## SPRING, AUSTRALIA, 1977

# Love is the Golden String

*"This rediscovery of religion is the great intellectual, moral and spiritual adventure of our time. It is something which calls for all our energies, and involves both labour and sacrifice . . . to be made by each individual . . . . find[ing] his own way through the labyrinth. But . . . . we cannot simply go back to the past . . . we have to make the discovery of God in the light of our modern knowledge, of all that physics, biology and psychology have to tell us. We have to see the significance of Christ in relation to the whole of that vast sphere of time which history and anthropology now open to us."*

Bede Griffiths, *The Golden String*, pp. 13-14

In his autobiography *The Golden String*, Bede Griffiths spoke of an experience he had during his final year at school. While he was walking one evening, the sun was setting over the playing fields. He wrote, "As I walked on I came upon some hawthorn trees in full bloom and again I thought that I had never seen such a sight or experienced such sweetness before." It was as though he had chanced upon the "Garden of Paradise" and in that moment, he recalled, "A lark rose suddenly from the ground . . . poured out its song above my head, and then sank still singing to rest." At this point, he remembered, a "feeling of awe" overcame him, such that even the sky seemed "but a veil before the face of God."

When I was appointed pastor to my first rural parish in 1976, it happened at a time in my life when I was enjoying what I judged to be some success and popularity in my work. I liked skimming along on the surface of life. As the reality of my new appointment sank in, however, I became disconcerted when I contemplated the looming prospect of years of isolation stretching ahead of me. It was then that through his books, I discovered Bede Griffiths. I started to write to him at his *ashram* in India. Among his many letters, there was one in which he urged me to seek "ways of discovering a sense of unity and meaning in the day-to-day experiences" of nature's wilderness in my part of the world. He exhorted me to listen to crows cawing and blowflies droning and to the sounds of silence. He urged me to stop and watch closely the heat hazes shimmering on the vast horizon, ancient landforms that host surprising flora and fauna, sun-baked soil that becomes unfriendly for seeds to flourish in, and floods that wash away hopes and dreams. He invited me to empathise with the farm families, who long to find their own sense of meaning in the intense and sometimes unforgiving isolation of the Australian Outback.

Mindful of this, I wanted to explore and find some spiritual guides in my experience, sources of wisdom that could help me bring the aura of the bush into my retreats as a spiritual director. I decided to go on several solo camping trips to the Fitzgerald River National Park. This enormous World Heritage wilderness was part of my parish. It is a land so depleted of natural minerals and trace elements that the plants growing there cannot survive elsewhere. They are as beautiful as they are strange. There is a shrub called the Bonsai Feather Flower, *verticordia oxylepis*. Though an extremely rare, protected Australian native plant, it looks like a wind-pruned, almost prostrate Japanese bonsai tree. Its delicately gnarled beauty, its rarity, and the species' hardiness and adaptability captivated me. Faced with such tenacity in clinging to life, I was elated that here in microcosm was the story of the cosmos. I'd tramp over fretting rocky breakaway ridges and cross wind-swept clay flats for hours, exploring the land and looking for some sign of the small outcrops here and there. I always headed for the most barren ground, the most exposed, for it is here in these places that the trees I sought would flourish as though imperishable. Once sighted, I would slow down. This was sacred ground, not a place to be rushed in upon clumsily or thoughtlessly. These trees and the land around were not mine to possess. My approach had, I felt, to be one of surrender. I would lie with stomach flat on the earth awed by the beauty I beheld. A small eddy of air might upset the delicate balance of life established so finely by this little outpost of the universe's urge to create, to give life and live. This incredibly remote, tiny copse of trees was, for me, as significant and meaningful as any of the world's great forests I'd ever visited. I was conscious of my need to walk gently and in silence here.

I find my thoughts and my daydreams returning to those years as a young pastor and spiritual director in the bush. I think that out there, I did in fact lay the foundations upon which I could build a sense of spirituality in daily life. I learnt with great difficulty and very slowly, that in my case, it has often been through suffering, and the surrender of what I imagined to be the good life that I found insight, peace, beauty and love. By walking this way, I have, in spite of failures, been more able to give love as well as meaningful insight to those with whom I have worked over the years.

Compared to my previous appointment, the new post was a wilderness of unpopularity and loneliness. This barren land of few parishioners and long, hard solitary miles in my hermitage-car could hardly keep a hitherto comfortable spirituality going. Very gradually, as the years progressed, this became a land that was tough enough to bring out, here and there, rugged plants of spiritual survival. I found a depth of soil in which friendships that stand the test of time could flourish here in an open, clean air that carries the experience, thoughts and hopes of a deeper unity to this cosmos. By their very existence and my sense of connectedness to them, those little *verticordia* forests in a remote Australian wilderness became my spiritual teachers.

**Father Bede's hut as viewed from one of the ashram's garden irrigation canals**

From his small *ashram* in South India, Bede Griffiths had also learned a way in which he could serve people, like me, who came to him for spiritual nourishment. He used to say that small is beautiful. He had courageously adapted to the Indian environment, thus including Hindu ritual as part of the Eucharist celebration. He wore the kavi habit of the Hindu *sannyasis*, he ate sitting on the floor and with his hands, and he walked barefoot. His example of 'littleness', simplicity and humility inspired many.

Father Bede assured me that the individual inner spiritual journey of discovery is "something that calls for all our energies, and involves both labour and sacrifice; each one approaches it from a different angle and has to work out his own particular problem. Each alike is given a golden string and has to find his way through the labyrinth." If, while at the *ashram*, I glanced into his room, on my way down the path near his hut around 2.30 a.m. in the pre-dawn, I would see him sitting deep in contemplation This was part of his several hours of preparation for the morning Eucharist.

For Bede Griffiths the "golden string" led from that evening at his school. He had to keep seeking and learning. He reported that, "every step in advance is a return to the beginning," and that the beauty to be found in nature, the cosmos, "is not only truth but also Love." Bede said that he discovered the divine, not only in the life of nature, but also in the minds and hearts of human beings. He found that he "sought the divine in the solitude of nature, and in the labour of his mind," but eventually found the answer in his community and the spirit of charity. Until then, he felt he had been "wandering in a far country and had returned home"; that he "had been dead and was alive again"; that he "had been lost and was [now] found."

What he did, he did not for himself, but for the love of God and the service of other people. Bede closed his autobiography with some words from the prior in Dostoevsky's novel *The Brothers Karamazov*. I feel these describe beautifully the way Bede tried to live his life for eighty-six years. "Love all God's creation, the whole and every grain of sand in it . . . If you love everything you will perceive the divine mystery in things. Once you perceive it, you will begin to comprehend it better every day. And you will come at last to love the whole world with an all-embracing love."

## Chapter 3

DRY SEASON, INDIA, 1984-1985

# Meditation as a Way of Self-transcendence

*"In meditation I can become aware of the ground of my being . . . . I can get beyond all these outer forms of things in time and space and discover the Ground from which they all spring . . . In each tradition the one divine Reality, the one eternal Truth, is present, but it is hidden under symbols . . . Always the divine Mystery is hidden under a veil, but each revelation (or 'unveiling') unveils some aspect of the one Truth . . . It is not by word or thought but by meditation on the Mystery that we can pierce the veil. This is where all human reason fails. All these words, Brahman, Nirvana, Allah, Yahweh, Christ, are meaningless to those who cannot get beyond their reason and allow the divine Mystery to shine through its symbol . . . It is this 'mystery of Christ' which lies at the heart of the gospels and of all the evolution of Christianity . . . And this Mystery when known in its ultimate ground is one with the mystery of Brahman, Nirvana, Tao, Yahweh, Allah. It is the one Truth, the one Word . . ."*

Bede Griffiths, *Return to the Centre*, pp. 36, 71, 73, 74

Early in 1984, after seven years in the bush, I took long service leave and headed for *Saccidananda ashram*. I was able to spend nearly six months with Father Bede. Each day I experienced his connectedness to the world of politics, economics, science, and mysticism. He was a man who maintained balance between too great an involvement in the mundane and too rarefied a position with regard to the otherworldly. He was, above all, a man for ordinary people. Bede could speak with the intellectual and scholarly, the powerful and worldly, as well as the humble, everyday person who came to the *ashram*, often with his or her own sufferings in tow. No day was the same as any other. Bede was always fresh and up-to-date with what was going on in the world. He related everything back to the mystery of God acting in the world and the need for a renewal of the contemplative life. As far as I was concerned in those days, it was the most exciting and yet the most peaceful and spiritually focused place on earth.

Around this time with Father Bede's encouragement, my companions, Sister Pascaline Coff and Brother Wayne Teasdale, and I departed on a series of rickety buses climbing laboriously up the Southern Ghats and across Karnataka State to visit SeraMe Buddhist Monastic University. Here eminent scholars teach their Tibetan Buddhist culture to thousands of students. The university lies south of Mysore, near the village of Bylakuppe, on land given to the Tibetan refugees by then Prime Minister Nehru. Conditions were primitive and crowded, but every monk seemed happy and contented. It was my first exposure to the Tibetan community in exile, the positive implications of which were to be profound in the coming years.

Just before Fr. Bede's seventy-eighth birthday on 11 December 1984, I rose early at 4.15 am, as custom demands at *Shantivanam*. I bathed in the communal shower block, ladling water over myself from a small hand jug from a larger tub. The *ashram* was still dark and utterly silent. Here and there people were making their way to their ablutions and then to the Temple for prayer and meditation. I had arranged to meet Father Bede on the banks of the sacred River Cauvery, the 'Ganges of the South', as it is called locally. Here, near the charnel grounds for the small village of Tannirpali, we performed the ceremonies required for taking oblation as a spiritual member of the *ashram* community. It was also the occasion for my reception, at Bede's hands, of *brahmacharya* or student-hood. This is the traditional Hindu period of 'dwelling in God', of 'moving in *Brahman*.'

Visitors to the *ashram* were conscious of the spirit of peace and meditation that provided the atmosphere in and around *Shantivanam*. Even the local Hindu farmers and villagers recognised this. They would stop at the small *ashram* temple to pray, even for a few minutes, before moving on to their various works by the river, among the coconut palm groves, or in the rice paddy fields. Bede never actually taught any systematic approach to meditation, though he was always meditating himself. To those who sought guidance,

Jesuit Fathers Ama Samy and Hugo Enomiya-Lassalles, India, 1984

such as myself, his teaching was clear and simple. He found the practice of meditation led him to a sense of 'flow,' providing him with a spiritual context in which he carried out his daily tasks.

# BEDE GRIFFITHS: FRIEND AND GIFT OF THE SPIRIT

During the Indian winter of 1985, Bede Griffiths received two Zen masters at the *ashram*. The older of the two was German Jesuit, Hugo Enomiya-Lassalles. His friend was an Indian of the same religious fraternity, Father Ama Samy. Having met and talked with them in the post-luncheon hours, when silence was not the rule, they and Dom Bede encouraged me to continue with them on their journey to Dindigal, further south in the state of Tamil Nadu. Here, I learned they'd be delivering a Zen *Sesshin*, an intense meditation retreat. I accepted their offer because some years before this, I had already completed a ten-day Buddhist *vipassana* meditation retreat in Thailand, and on another occasion, I went through the process under the strict guidance of the Burmese teacher Sri S. N. Goenka. Father Bede, though not a practitioner of Zen meditation, extracted a small piece of paper from his scrapbook. He presented it to me as something for the coming retreat. In his own handwriting he had copied the "Four Zen Vows" that are customarily taken by participants on *Sesshin*.

> Though beings are numberless, I vow to awaken with them
> Though delusions are inexhaustible, I vow to end them
> Though Dharma gates are boundless, I vow to enter them
> Though Buddha's way is unsurpassable, I vow to become it

After collecting a few clothes and toiletries in an overnight backpack, I found myself in the front seat of an old but sturdy Ambassador car, hurtling in the direction of Dindigal, and the looming strict discipline of the *Sesshin*.

Enomiya-Lassalles was a man of evident scholarship, deep prayer and asceticism. An unusually tall man, he conducted himself with a quiet, serious disposition. He might have looked severe as he walked through the *ashram* compound, in his long black Jesuit robe. But his eyes shone, giving a light to his face that gave

## Meditation as a Way of Self-transcendence

an air of gentleness and quiet wisdom. He had taken up Zen meditation some time after the Second World War. As a German and Jesuit, he was in Nagasaki when the atomic bomb exploded there in 1945. He maintained the belief that the practice of Zen was his way of understanding the soul of Japan more effectively. His hope was that through his teaching of Zen meditation in Europe, he might help Westerners ameliorate the effects of the materialistic and mechanistic conditions in which modern people live. The two teachers said very little to each other and hardly spoke to me at all. I tried to introduce small talk, but soon realised they were two deliberately silent, thoughtful men for whom superficial conversation held little value. Nevertheless, I felt relaxed and comfortable in their company and looked forward to the days ahead.

Our Ambassador clattered into Dindigal. We were exhausted from the heat of the journey, and after sharing a small meal with the rest of the participants, we retired to our rooms for a good night's sleep. There was a demanding schedule to be maintained for the coming week. For approximately sixteen hours every day (two meals and exercise excepted), almost the sole occupation was simply to sit on a cushion and meditate on the passing nature of each moment. Every physical and mental event was noted as arising, observed as dispassionately as possible, and then let go. Relief was provided daily in a period of *dokusan*, going in single-file for an interview with Father Lassalles, in order to receive direction. The purpose of *dokusan* is to keep the student's mind from going astray during the many hours of sitting. I liked lining up with the other participants in the darkened corridor. Just standing was a welcome relief. Eventually, I knew when it was my turn. A small bell rang from inside the teacher's room. Upon entry I sat, as directed, within twelve inches of his cushion, facing him directly. It was a shock to be so close and to feel so vulnerable in the presence of Father Lassalles, who was manifestly wiser and more experienced than I. This sort of situation is specifically designed as a central part of any *Sesshin*. It had the potential to sweep away any pretence of my reliance on words or the intellect. By simply looking into my eyes, I felt Father Lassalles knew intuitively whether there was progress or not. Some students of other Zen teachers have undergone the experience of being shouted at, or even hit. This didn't happen to me. But for those who have been so confronted, the intention is to frighten the student out of his or her interior darkness, into the sudden light, as Father Lassalles said, "rather like a spark shooting out from striking flint."

The heat of South India was more intense than anything I'd previously experienced. It was already a major focus of my complaining mind and body at *Shantivanam*. In a car accident on the way to India, I had sustained injury to my ribs. I was uncomfortable for weeks. Father Bede had taken pity on me, making sure that I was well looked after. He provided me with a small stool instead of the bare floor, and gave me a thin mattress instead of the concrete bench most ashramites slept on. He even arranged with the nearby village for me to have one egg each day for breakfast "to keep up your strength," he said. I was thankful for small mercies. The situation in Dindigal was altogether different. Father Lassalles was a man of imposing self-discipline. I feel he expected the same mental and physical attitude from those attending his *Sesshin*. Pain, fatigue and hunger seemed, for me anyway, to be the only realities in the entire universe. When, finally, fatigue and loss of concentration overtook me or others sitting in the meditation room, it would become obvious in body language.

Unseen by anyone, as we all had our faces to the wall, Father Ama Samy would quietly come round and tap one on the shoulder with a long flattened wooden stick called the Sword of Manjusri — the Sword of Compassion. This, he would lift over his shoulder and suddenly bring down on the student's sagging shoulder. Strangely, everyone in the room benefited from the loud 'thwack', and each

**Father Ama Samy, Jesuit Zen Master (Roshi)**

wondered if they'd be next! Both posture and concentration were definitely better after that. Yet altogether, through these experiences, I gradually saw how simple life could be when simplicity is expected of me. Most of what I demanded of life tended to be 'extras' and often decorative, rather than essential; so few things are really essential. I discovered what I most required for an ordinary, reasonably balanced life was to be modestly comfortable and pain-free, able to sleep when tired, and with enough food to live healthily in the performance of my duties. On the other hand, through the painful experiences associated with the retreat process, I learnt how automatic and addictive my responses to events and circumstances in everyday life had become.

During the intensive meditation process and together with other people, I observed several personal addictions. These included aversion to discomfort and pain of almost any sort; the craving for pleasure and comfort in its many delectable varieties; and the tuning out from "neutral" or boring experiences — things, events, and people that merely disinterested one. All three of these experiences were, in turn, comprised in the passing moments of that retreat. I sensed that my life, cluttered with its many, often pointless activities, was anything but balanced and simple. I had become anxious about many things that were, by and large, not essential for my happiness. Despite trying to hold the balance and embodying this aspiration by attendance at demanding meditation retreats over the years, I have sometimes observed how remarkably unsuccessful I seem to have been. But I do support myself by the realisation that spiritual achievement is not a goal, but a journey. I'm certainly not there yet, and I have far to go. I remember Father Bede declaring a similar sentiment in the last year of his life.

*Saccidananda ashram* had become a centre for inter-religious dialogue. Fr. Bede lived what he preached in this matter. Whether welcoming Mahayana Buddhist monks from Tibet, or Zen Buddhist monks from Japan, or Theravadan monks from Thailand and Sri Lanka or Burma, as well as Hindu swamis and yogis, or Christians of various denominations, Bede was always engaged respectfully in dialogue that sought to refresh and guide his own spiritual development as well as be an example for the guests staying at any given time in *Shantivanam*. During the more than thirty years he spent in India, Bede Griffiths understood the transforming experience of inter-religious dialogue. He well understood how this could be very challenging for those who fearfully cling to what Judson Trapnell calls the "distinctions that separate person from person and tradition from tradition." Trapnell opines that it is necessary for those who engage in such dialogue to undergo a self-transcendence, "beyond familiar habits of thinking." Bede was also aware of the cost that profound and committed immersion in such waters could demand. In his openness to others, and detachment from his cultural and religious biases, he lived what he proposed. Participants in serious inter-religious dialogue recognise a greater wholeness and are opened to truth as found through persons and symbols beyond their own culture and religion. In a paper on transcending dualism, Bede wrote that we "have to meditate and open ourselves to the transcendent reality." To work, merely on the rational level, prevents any solid advance. He urged openness to the place of meeting, where the transcendent dwells, in the depth of the human heart. Here it is, he said, that "the Jew, the Christian, the Moslem, the Hindu and the Buddhist open themselves in prayer and in meditation, to the transcendent mystery, going beyond the word, beyond thought, simply opening themselves to the light, to the truth, to reality, then the meeting takes place. That is where humanity will be united. Only through transcendence can we find unity."

# Chapter 4
## DRY SEASON, INDIA, 1985
# The Practice of the Presence of God

*"I had been used to ordinary kindness and family affection, but I had never known a charity which was based on principle and pervaded the most ordinary acts of life. Here was that kind of courtesy and grace... which had... its source in the Rule of St Benedict. 'Let all guests who come,' it was said, 'be treated like Christ himself...' This was the sign for which I had been seeking."*

Bede Griffiths, The Golden String, p. 132-133

In January of 1985, Father Bede was excited by the developments in Eastern Europe. Every day at the Eucharist, he offered commentary on what was unfolding, especially during his elocution at midday prayer. He viewed the collapse of the old Soviet Union in the same way as he viewed the ordinary, historical structures of the church throughout the centuries. Indeed, he saw human institutions generally, as "subject to all the vicissitudes of time and space". Even the church, which began as an inspiration of God, he asserted, "Becomes overshadowed by human sins and infirmity . . . by human limitations, cultural blindness, narrowness of mind, and fanaticism." He saw that the Soviet Union's destiny was, if it would survive at all, the same as that of the church: to "find new forms of expression", so that it might become more relevant to the world in which it lives. Speaking of the church, the need to open ourselves to the truth in all religions, was, for Bede, an absolute necessity, one that requires a rediscovery of its essential truth as well as a painful rejection of its cultural and historical limitations. Bede saw the contemporary world as entering "a time of trial", one in which mankind must ask whether it will continue "to build up [the] scientific world [through armaments and unbridled consumption], or will mankind learn to repent, to turn back, to rediscover the source of life, the Wisdom of Mother Earth." For Bede this wisdom is also the wisdom of the East.

Father Bede expressed understandable delight, when towards the end of 1986, Pope John Paul II called an historic meeting, where participants from the world's religions could pray for peace. He recognised that the Pope wanted to prove that peace is the desire of people of all faiths; that peace ultimately is possible. On the feast of St. Francis the Pope had strongly suggested a world truce for October 27, "asking that guns be silent for the day and conflicts suspended. A good number of countries heeded his call: chiefs of state issued messages and declarations in favor of peace, urging their constituents to reflect on peace; it is reported that prayer meetings for peace were held in many countries."

In the middle of 1985, Father Bede travelled to Australia together with his companion of many years, Swami Amaldas, for his first national tour. Amaldas, a competent yogi, conducted popular *yoga* workshops. Father Bede spoke to thousands in person, on radio and television. He addressed his audiences with a constant message: the importance of a marriage of East and West, the interface of Western Science and Eastern Mysticism. In these he stressed the importance of a renewal of the contemplative life and prayer for a more peaceful world. Throughout his national tour, Father Bede's un-self-conscious intention was to embody spirituality. His practice

**Father Bede with Swami Amaldas, Perth, Western Australia, 1985**

of the presence of God also had the capacity to open hearts and transform people and situations. Many still speak of the significance of that visit and its continued effect on their lives.

In the mid-1960s I entered a Hindu temple in Singapore. It was my first journey overseas, one that introduced me to the richness and profundity of 'The East'. Just as I moved through the crowd of devotees, pressing around the entrance to this place, a bare-chested Brahmin priest raised a fresh coconut above his head and dashed it to pieces at my feet. It was a startling occurrence. I'd never seen a public display of religion, let alone one that took such an explosive turn. Some of the young people who were there, seeing my amazement, came to me afterwards and explained the ritual. As a result of their openhearted friendliness and eagerness to help me understand what I'd witnessed, we shared a meal and established a lifelong friendship that I renew when I visit the island.

Some years later, I was to find that same ritual enacted at *Saccidananda ashram* – the *ashram* of the Holy Trinity. Its significance was symbolic for me at this time, and Bede's explanation of the nearby village temple bridged the years:

> At the entrance of the temple is the figure of the god Ganesh, the elephant god . . . his fundamental characteristic is his power to remove obstacles . . . Whenever (devotees) want to undertake a journey . . . they pray to Ganesh to remove the obstacles. So on entering a temple they break a coconut before the shrine of Ganesh . . . a beautiful action. A coconut has a hard, rough exterior, but inside there is a white substance and sweet milk. The outer nutshell is the external self, the ego (i.e., devotees break their ego). Inside is the pure white substance, the sweet milk, symbolizing the divine life within. So they try to remove all obstacles from the mind and make it open to God.

That is the first stage of opening the heart, of embodying spirituality, and of transforming one's own heart, as well as potentially touching other hearts.

Following daily rituals and movements, I settled into a rhythm made possible by the lifestyle and inner-directedness of Father Bede and the *ashram* community. Together, they created an environment that honoured the individual's journey to the true Self. By this is meant the Self that is deeper and more essentially oneself than one's ego consciousness. During my time at the *ashram*, I experienced a gradual breaking of the outer shell of the ego, of selfishness and superficiality.

Here and there, in the performance of my pastoral ministry, I had become, I think, satisfied with mechanically 'performing a duty', without a real sense of meaning and self-transcendence. However, meditating and conversing with Bede had the potential for bringing

**The author as principle celebrant of the Eucharist and Father Bede, Saccidananda ashram temple, 1985**

me to the centre and recovering meaning in my life. Meaning, I found, is everywhere: in symbols and in specific experiences, though the meaning attached to symbols and experiences is often not easily articulated. Among these experiences are believing in God and maintaining personal values. I see the search for meaning as one of the fundamental issues of our times. It becomes manifest in questions, such as what is life all about? What does my job mean? What does this company or non-profit corporation that I have founded, or work for, mean to me? What does this relationship mean for me, and why remain committed? Why am I studying for this diploma or degree? What does it mean to be me? What does it mean that I am going to die one day? The reasons people seek answers to these and other questions are not merely rational, nor are they wholly emotional. It seems to me people have an innate sense of wanting to find value and that element of "something more" in their lives.

Bede Griffiths would often refer to several contemporary scientists' views of Newtonian science, which draws sharp distinctions between the observing 'subject' — the individual — and the observed 'object.' He felt there was little place in Newton's physics for mind or consciousness, or as an example, for the human struggle to find meaning and endurance, and the human desire to rise above negative circumstances and transcend limits. Newtonian philosophy speaks of a deterministic, objective universe, in which the strict laws of motion and gravitation govern everything. These laws render everything predictable, without the element of surprise. In this 'mechanistic' world-view, humans are pushed around as helpless bystanders, as isolated, passive cogs in a clockwork machine. Bede's point was that such a 'mechanistic' view of the world ignores the insight that human beings are 'more than the sum total of their parts.' The mechanistic view reduces the individual to the status of a 'fragmented object' in a senseless, though highly organised, predictable cosmos. Ultimately, death is also viewed by many as terrifying because of the lack of any meaningful context for the natural ending of this life with grace and peace. In relation to this state of affairs, Bede would refer to the written works of modern quantum physicists and poets. But he also enjoyed and often read from the works of the British author D. H. Lawrence, who in his poem *Healing* speaks of a world view that treats people as machines:

> I am not a mechanism, an assembly of various sections.
> And it is not because the mechanism is working
>     wrongly that I am ill.
> I am ill because of wounds to the soul, to the deep
>     emotional self

and the wounds to the soul take a long, long time, only
    time can help
and patience, and a certain difficult repentance
long, difficult repentance, realisation of life's mistake,
    and freeing oneself
from the endless repetition of this mistake
which mankind at large has chosen to sanctify.

Visitors who came to the *ashram* often brought their wounds with them. Under his guidance, Bede helped many recover their sense of wholeness. Some needed longer than others, but each was given according to their need of Bede's kindness, patience and compassion. From the industrial, mechanised Western world in particular, people would have a chance to recognise their always-existing inner beauty. For most that found their way to *Shantivanam*, their path was reported as a journey to the centre. The very design of the *ashram* spoke of the progressive nature of this Journey. The road of life was symbolised by the long, dusty track leading from the main road to the front gates of the *ashram*. The lotus-covered water tank near the temple symbolises cleansing from sin. The temple bell suspended from a shady, overarching tree near the forecourt is a symbol of the sudden wakening of the inner consciousness. It rings when the doors of the inner temple open wide to the love of God. "Wake up!" it tolls. "Become aware! He awaits you!" There is a small lamp burning perpetually in the temple. To give light, three elements are necessary: the lamp, the oil and the wick. If one of these is neglected or removed, there is darkness. Our human body is the lamp, our mind is the oil, and our tongue is the wick. To have peace, joy and love, all three must be kept trimmed. At the end of prayer and various *ashram* rituals, there is a waving of lights, called the *arati*. Camphor, a fragrant substance, denoting the fragrance of the Spirit, is burnt. The light produced symbolically grants enlightenment to those sharing it. *Arati* teaches us to burn in love for the sake of others. The great banyan tree at the centre of the *ashram* is the symbol of that Eternal Tree, with its roots firmly planted in heaven. And the lush gardens that lead, by circuitous routes, to the heart of the *ashram*, together with the temple, are a sign of the gardens of paradise to enjoy here and now. All of these elements come together, said Bede, so as to bring the Journeyer to a central point:

> [That point is within the temple and is called] the *garbha griha*, the 'house of the womb,' the source of life, or the *mulasthanam*, the inner sanctuary, which is always dark. The meaning of this is that God, the ultimate mystery, dwells in darkness, beyond the light of this world. In the little temple in our *ashram* we follow the same pattern: the inner sanctuary is always kept in darkness with only an oil lamp burning before the tabernacle. So going to the temple means leaving the outer world behind,

Tabernacle in the 'garbha griha' — womb-house, Saccidananda ashram, 1985

going through purification, uniting with all the powers of the cosmos and finally entering into the inner shrine of the Self where God dwells in the darkness. At that point one experiences union with God.

The patterns that emerge from a regular life of quiet prayer and reflective work often clarify and guide, as well as instruct, the way forward. I was always aware of abundant synchronicity in the day-to-day activities of the *ashram*. Building on the daily program and ambience, individuals in the community would often, through a word or conversation or by an example of prayerfulness, be the means whereby others found an answer or a signpost for forward movement. In *ashram* life, the old familiar landscape would sometimes buckle. New realities would stand out, and familiar perspectives would recede. *Shantivanam* became a place where people might find 'the will of God.' Bede would advise that this will can only be known "by trying and making mistakes." Over time a perception of continual guidance would be discerned. He referred to one of the central activities of life at *Shantivanam* as meditation. In this important activity, Bede would say, the meditator is "guided to meet the right people, to go to the right place, to do the right thing, and see that [they] are not managing [their] life just by [themselves]. God is acting in [them]. . . We are part of the rhythm of the universe. Once we tune into it, things begin to happen . . . if we are attentive and watchful and flow with that rhythm, then we do [what is] right and are moved by the Spirit."

## Chapter 5

### DRY SEASON, INDIA, 1986-1987

# The Indian Stages of Life

*"I began to realise that it was possible to follow Christ . . . the greater part of his life had been spent in complete obscurity at Nazareth. I saw now that this hidden life, spent in a small village away from the world, among peasants and small craftsmen, was a model of the life of every Christian . . ."*

Bede Griffiths, *The Golden String, p. 133*

In 1987 Catholic Sisters Vandana Mataji and Ishpriya Mataji toured Australia for their first visit. They delivered lectures and retreats during the beautiful Western Australian wildflower season, September and October. They were both experienced yogis and close friends and colleagues of Father Bede. With him, they were part of the small but highly motivated Christian *ashram* movement in India. Their small "Jeevan Dhara", or Living Waters *ashram*, perched on a spur of the Himalayan foothills, near Lansdowne and Rishikesh, was, like *Saccidananda ashram*, a place of inter-religious dialogue. Here, members of all faiths could gather for prayer and meditation, as well as conversation and sharing at the deepest level on matters of spiritual importance. People came to experience silence and learn meditation and *yoga*. As with Father Bede, they acknowledged the thousands of Westerners who travelled to India seeking God. India could make this offering in a way that was not readily available in their home countries. Vandana and Ishpriya joined Father Bede in the *ashram* movement. They created their *ashram* as a place of solitude and simplicity. Here, people could work manually, intellectually and spiritually in an open community lifestyle, as though at an oasis in an otherwise parched desert. Their goal was not so much to transform structures of the Church, though indirectly this would always be a possibility, as it was to provide encouragement and the means of transformation within the individual person.

There is a view which asserts that human development is a mechanistic progression rather than an unfolding, which continues uninterrupted throughout life. The mechanistic view tends to rule out the possibility that at a certain stage, there could be a deviation from the 'normal production-line' view of the life journey. Over many centuries in India, society has built itself upon the fact that people go through developmental or unfolding stages. There are rituals and celebrations honouring each stage the individual successfully negotiates and the next to which he or she now looks.

The term 'asrama' is derived from the root 'srama', which means 'to exert oneself,' as well as the *place* and *mode* of exertion. It signifies the place where one lives, and the stage in the journey of life. In this world individuals are on a quest for God. In India, this was schematised into four stages or 'stop-overs' on the pilgrimage to eternity. The journey's theme is one of the great archetypal themes of world literature, influencing spiritual and cultural practices found through the four life stages or *asramas* of India.

Scholar and friend of Bede Griffiths, Jesu Rajan explains that *brahmacharya*, or student-hood, is the period of 'dwelling in God'; of 'moving in *Brahman*.' This is the time, beginning at the age of twelve, in which society gives the best of its heritage to an individual. The period lasts for about twelve years under the guidance of a competent *guru*.

This time of continence, frugality and self-discipline ends with a ritual, which frees the young man from the student life, so as to begin the life of a householder.

*Grhastha* is the period becoming a householder life. The individual now helps propagate the human species by raising a family and assists in the cultural development of society. Every aspect of virtuous social conduct is considered: from offering of daily prayers, to the duties of hospitality, charity, industry, honesty, generosity, purity in all matters, and truthfulness.

*Vanaprastha*, or semi-retirement from life, in which the person undertakes a more intense quest for the Absolute, may, for some, even take the form of forest-dweller. Now freed from the cares of worldly living, the seeker pursues purely spiritual aims. This is the period of life in which there is a further development of the values – patience in hardship, friendliness to fellow humans, and compassion towards all living creatures. Once a day the seeker eats only vegetarian food. It is the time for meditation and study of the scriptures. Consistent with *ashram* culture, this mode of life was offered without impediment at *Shantivanam*. Those who could not accept this regime, soon left and returned to other occupations. There was no disgrace in this. It was accepted as a phase of their journey. Those however, who did stay in retirement, would serve society by offering guidance to others.

Should an individual live as long, the final period of life, that of *sannyasa*, is one of total renunciation and detachment. Herein the individual retires totally, seeking to know, find and realize the Spirit or Self that hides within the core of his being.

Each of these *asramas*, or stages, is a time of training and preparation for the next stage of gradually intensifying asceticism. The person is purified of attachments, thus becoming fit for self-realization, that is, for freedom. Living with the bare necessities of life is the path of great renunciation, a constant reminder to society of the supreme goal of human existence. The *sannyasi* declares: "I have given up everything." A new set of simple, mud coloured clothing, a staff and a begging bowl is all they own. They are given a sacred *mantra*, or prayer word, as a point of reference for meditation and contemplation. Theirs is now the life of poverty, simplicity, solitude and silence, with the practice of universal love and prayerfulness, seeing everything in the universe as a manifestation of God. For *sannyasis*, nothing is seen as either better or worse than anything else.

**Memorials to the founders Fathers Henri Le Saux and Jules Monchinin, Temple forecourt, Saccidananda ashram**

Bede's predecessor at *Shantivanam* was the French Benedictine Henri Le Saux, known as Swami Abhishiktananda. He believed that the natural place for the Christian to celebrate the renunciation involved in all the *asramas* of life will be within the Eucharist – Jesus' gift of himself for the sake of all. There are Gospel readings in which Jesus summons his disciples to complete renunciation and the way of the Cross:

The Son of Man has nowhere to lay his head . . .
Go, sell what you have . . . and come, follow me . . .
Leave the dead to bury the dead . . .
No man who puts his hand to the plough and looks back,
is fit for the Kingdom of God.
If anyone does not 'hate' his father, mother, wife, children . . .
even his own life, he cannot be my disciple.
Take nothing for your journey — no staff, bag, bread, money,
no change of clothes . . .
>   (Luke 9:58; Mark 10:21; Luke 9:62; 14:26; 9:3; etc.)

In today's India, these traditions are being modified. The tradition of householders undertaking the forest-dweller's life is diminishing, as are those who take on *sannyasa*. But the kernel remains, as does the ultimate goal of living as witnesses to the transcendence of God. On some occasions, Bede would welcome visiting *sannyasis* to *Shantivanam*. Their presence was always appreciated and regarded as significant. He would devote part of his day in dialogue with such figures when they passed through alone or with a small retinue of followers.

Westerners have no tradition of such strict categories of social and personal spiritual development. Nevertheless, there is a firm and long standing tradition of renunciation in the West that may be undertaken to ensure the building of strong communities. Perchance the first place that the rebuilding of community, if it is recognised as a value, can start may be in the individual decision to take up the quiet and hidden daily practice of meditation. In my experience, to build community requires deep insight and understanding, willingness to listen, and an open heart. In essence, a life of contemplation is to see and relate to reality in all its parts, and to relate to reality as it is. Such an attitude eschews discrimination. Beyond the rational, intellectual processes, and beyond tired, worn out concepts and language, contemplation is a "whole way of life" said Father Bede. He sometimes referred to D. H. Lawrence, whose works he admired. In his scrapbook, Bede had hand written some words of Laurence's:

> Whoever wants the world to be perfect, should take the precaution of having no real likes or dislikes. Universal good will is all one can allow oneself.

## Chapter 6
### DRY SEASON, INDIA, 1988-1989
# Finding Spirituality in the Ordinary

*"I wanted to find a life which would satisfy my whole being, my heart and soul and body as well as my mind."*

Bede Griffiths, *The Golden String*, p. 132

In September of 1989, Indian Jesuit Father Ama Samy, an acknowledged Zen Master or Roshi, visited Western Australia for the first time. He was conducting Zen Sesshin, as well as a number of lectures explaining the Zen Buddhist method of Zazen, or "sitting meditation". As Father Bede's friend, I had met Ama Samy in India at *Shantivanam*, sat with him and German Jesuit Zen Master Enomiya Lassalles, and had, as an element of my ongoing work in the field of inter-religious dialogue, given them the invitation to travel to Australia. Father Ama Samy, though a Catholic priest of many years, saw himself as an Asian, bringing this form of Buddhism back to its original home in India. Through his commitment and loyalty to the inner search, together with the encouragement of religious colleagues such as Father Bede, he found a fruitful ministry in bringing Zen retreats to seekers throughout India, as well as, over a number of visits, to Australia in the following years.

*Saccidananda ashram* is on the banks of the sacred River Cauvery, near the South Indian settlement of Tannirpali, and is like a small village. It has extensive flower gardens and crops, a few beasts of burden, and a small herd of dairy cows. There are coconut groves, water wells, and irrigation channels criss-crossing the fields and gardens. All these need constant care and attention if the community is to flourish in a self-sufficient manner. Before dawn, an elderly widow sweeps the leaves from the paths that must be kept free from litter. Sometimes she finds a stray mango, which she is happy to share with *ashram* guests. While the *ashram's* permanent community and paid staff start work at dawn, guests don't contribute their labour until after breakfast. Everyone, no matter what his or her station in life, is expected, for an hour or two, to offer some form of practical work in

Library designed by Father Bede, Saccidananda ashram

the gardens, fields, workshops, or library. I would enjoy peeling and cutting the vegetables for the day's lunch. Such undemanding tasks

*Finding Spirituality in the Ordinary*

**Father Bede welcomed to the ashram community's celebrations for his birthday, 1988**

presented all who participated with an opportunity to share travellers' tales, jokes and laughter. It was an excellent way to build community and keep two feet on the ground.

Because an *ashram* community is so close to the natural rhythms of Nature and Hindu village society, I could see the way everything is related to the sacred. Nothing is undertaken or completed without some ritual sacrifice. Father Bede would often arrange for local Hindu craftsmen to come and erect buildings. For instance, the *ashram* library, which he designed, with special attention to the roof of typical village tiles, is a notable feature. Firstly, the builder has to select the auspicious day and hour of commencement. The land is then blessed and the workmen situate themselves in relation to the cosmos, that is, in relation to God and the cosmic powers and in relation to their neighbours. Then, before they get under way, they seek a blessing on their labour. Nothing happens until the work is consecrated. This is a sign that without God, no work is undertaken or completed. There is another blessing when the work is almost done. Father Bede told how local village meetings begin with prayer; and, if there are books of account to be presented, the corners of these too are daubed with sacred sandal wood paste as a consecration.

In India, every aspect of life is ordered to the world beyond, to the Infinite. In December 1988 I attended Bede's birthday celebrations. Long before dawn, everyone who in some way served the *ashram* community, including guests, calmly busied themselves with preparations, as though putting themselves, the community, and the whole of *Shantivanam*, the 'Forest of Peace', in harmony with the universe. Everyone dressed in his or her best clothes and all were set to enjoy the music and carnival atmosphere. Some of the musicians had travelled all night by bus to perform. Preparations included the prayer and ritual, all arrangements for the visiting guests, such as water purification and cooking of the food. Decorations were made from bamboo leaves and these were hung from every available branch, door lintel, and ceiling. Flowers bedecked statues, sacred objects, and prayer books. It seemed every nook and cranny of the *ashram* had a flower decorating it. Auspicious symbols, created from finely ground rice flour, were traced out on the ground in the temple forecourt and throughout the *ashram*. Each person contributed what art he or she was skilled in with the utmost care. For the whole day it seemed that everyone smiled. One of the many colourful aspects of the day was the luncheon, joined in by over a thousand villagers and their children. After the Eucharistic ceremonies, the whole gathering of ashramites and villagers, Hindu and Christian, Indian, and visiting foreigners, commenced lunch by acknowledging that food is a gift from God. Father Bede was never far away and could be seen to be personally involved in this or that tiniest aspect

*Finding Spirituality in the Ordinary*

Left: Local villagers (1000+) enjoy lunch on Father Bede's birthday, 1988
Right: Fathers Bede and Christudas enjoy cutting the birthday cake, 1988

of the preparations though it wasn't for long, as the many visitors claimed his ear and soon had him sitting down on some log or low garden wall listening to their story.

In the Hindu tradition, banana leaves are placed on the ground before each guest. The guest sprinkles water around the leaves to purify and make that space sacred. They may also wave incense over the food. This practice is called *arati*, signifying the offering of air. It is an extension of what happens at the Eucharist in the Indian rite. The altar, the physical and invisible surroundings and the people, are all sprinkled with water to purify and make the place sacred. Upon the banana leaves, each guest would take his or her meal. First came the boiled white rice, then the dhal, vegetables, curds and some fruit. In Father Bede's understanding: "Food comes to us from God, as part of the cosmic order. It is given to us to feed our life. Eating becomes a sacrifice, an offering of food in the fire of the stomach to the Spirit within."

Eventually Father Bede sat at his place, surrounded by hundreds of guests. Each year more than a thousand would gather for the celebrations. Everyone would be fed as an integral part of the day's festivities. After intoning the prayer of thanks and prayers of offering of the food, he quietly consumed his meal. I was always impressed by the way he exercised custody of the eyes — doubtless a remnant of his monastic discipline as part of daily life in England. Occasionally he would lift his gaze, and with evident enjoyment, he watched his many friends enjoy meal. Neither the ceremonies nor the meal were hurried; the *ashram* community served each person with grace and dignity. The supreme moment came when he cut his enormous, colourfully decorated birthday cake. It was then cut into pieces. Everyone lined up to take a portion, as though from Father Bede's hand, it was *prasad*, a gift from God. For each piece of cake, like every part of the whole meal, was food that has been offered to God.

Each December 17th over the thirty years that Bede celebrated his birthday at the *ashram*, guests of every station in life, every nationality or religion were welcomed with grace and ease. Nothing was rushed. No person felt they were more or less important than their neighbour. Father Bede and the *ashram* community received each guest as God himself. It was a powerful lesson: an example of what may happen when people come together to celebrate the life of a good and holy man.

Father Bede manifested divine presence within and through the performance of his daily tasks with such grace and ease that strangers felt warmly welcomed. Happiness is not in more; it is in less; not less contribution, but less of one's ego, and more of oneself as authentic being. It is in caring for and contributing to others.

# Chapter 7

### DRY SEASON, INDIA, 1990-1991

# Contemplation as a Whole Way of Life

*"Something has to come into human nature from above it, and it is that . . . which can release us and set us free. So the process is one of going beyond the mind to the Self that is within . . . The external battle has been left behind. At the beginning Arjuna is represented as being engaged in an external battle, but the real battle is internal. His fight is against the enemy of the soul; to destroy desire is the real object, not to destroy enemies on the battle field. To kill the enemy within, the force [that] is killing the true Self."*

Bede Griffiths, River of Compassion, p. 61

Bede Griffiths discovered the Hindu scriptures as a young man. A friend of his mother introduced them to him. Most significant were the *Bhagavad Gita*, the Song of the Lord; the *Dhammapada*, the Buddha's Way of Virtue; and the *Sayings* of Lao Tzu. He wrote in his autobiography: "The influence of these books upon my life was later to be immense, and I still look on them as the three greatest books of spiritual wisdom outside the New Testament . . ." I have seen the markings he made in the margins of one of these books. For, along with his few clothes and personal effects, he brought the *Gita*, carefully wrapped, in his multi-coloured shoulder bag to Australia during his visits of 1985 and 1992. He said that as a result of reading these books, the influence of Eastern tenet on his life and thought "remained an undercurrent to the present day."

Bede understood the powers that work against human freedom. In particular, he spoke of the desire that humans have for more and more power and control over their own lives and the lives of others. Sometimes the exaggerated character of this desire is a cause of major conflict in a person's life, precipitating a crisis in which one is thrust out of all that once seemed safe, secure, and manageable. He addressed such issues in daily talks in the *ashram*. Bede showed the *Bhagavad Gita* as a rich source of guidance for people suffering conflict in their lives. He referred to the spiritual seeker, who, at a time of personal spiritual crisis, is driven out of his familiar world, as the Israelites were driven out of Egypt, to wander in the desert for forty years. Toward the end of the desert period, he writes in his commentary on the *Gita*, the *River of Compassion*, a point comes for the Israelites, when the powers of the spirit seem to disappear altogether. At this point the powers of matter, the demonic powers, seem to be in control. That is, he writes, precisely the situation with the *Pandavas*, those heroes of the *Gita*, who are attempting to regain their throne, and who are preparing for a great battle against the *Kauravas*, the usurpers of the kingdom. For the *Pandavas* have been through what might be called the 'dark night of the soul,' and now, in their newfound sense of integrity, they cannot come to an agreement with the usurpers. "This," said Bede "is a very significant point, symbolizing that agreement can never be reached at the level of the human soul, because the soul itself is tragically divided against itself."

It is ever thus. And so, on the battlefield, Prince Arjuna sees the great tragedy: that his enemies (i.e., his afflictive emotions) are in fact, his friends and relatives. He is overwhelmed when he realizes that he is divided against himself. That is the human predicament.

In the battle of life we are divided against ourselves. There is no solution on the human level. It is only when *Krishna* the Spirit, the Lord, begins to counsel Arjuna that an answer can be found.

The prince, like anyone in similar circumstances, is in despair, for he realizes, as he looks out over the battlefield that he will have to begin making some hard decisions. Arjuna says: "I shall have to kill all these, my relatives and friends." When the spiritual journey is seriously embarked, much of the past will have to be relinquished. We have become comfortable, even secure, with the existing order of our lives. But we understand that we can't be free and come home to our true self until we surrender to a Higher Power. Additionally, there will typically be powerful new temptations arising with which we need to do battle. This is the problem, wrote Bede:

> When we are asked to give up the world and to fight against our instincts, passions, and desires, it looks as though there is nothing left and it seems as if one is in a desert. This highlights one of the perennial problems of the spiritual life. We give up Egypt, we give up the world and the pleasures of the senses, we give up appearances and go out into the desert. Our state then is that we have lost the world but we do not seem to have gained anything. That is why Arjuna is in despair . . .

For Bede the answer was very clear: what we have to learn is that on the human level, there is no answer to the problems of life. Again, he wrote in his book *River of Compassion:* "We recognise that we are driven by unconscious forces which cannot be controlled . . . we are not fully aware of what we are doing . . . we act unwillingly, as if we had no power to resist." The answer is found, he observed, when "we go beyond our ego, beyond ourself," and the Spirit within begins to speak. At that grace-filled moment, when "we are in a state which we cannot get out of by ourselves," we must be prepared to listen.

# BEDE GRIFFITHS: FRIEND AND GIFT OF THE SPIRIT

At *Shantivanam*, Father Bede often spoke of the demonic forces that act against the discipline of practicing the presence of God. He was convinced of the need that we all have to recognise our propensity for assuming positions of power and control over others, who, for whatever reason, are seen as different. He maintained that human beings everywhere have this temptation. Likewise, he noted the passion and attachment which human beings can develop for specific results in their own life or for a favourite cause.

The issues involved in the surrendering of power and control over what may well have become the disaster of our individual lives extend also to greater theatres of struggle. One day while having afternoon tea, we all sat together in the *ashram* rotunda. Father Bede was with us. He spoke of the way in which some nations in the West and even some authorities within the Church seemed to find the need for power and control to be indispensable. This need was sometimes disguised as "doing good" for others. He told a story as follows: "The Church in India is rightfully renowned for its charity. A priest friend of mine once asked a local Hindu villager what he thought of Christians. The Hindu gentleman said: 'I think you are all very good people, and I admire all your good works. But I cannot see you have any religion!'" At first we were a little shocked. We remained hushed. But then we laughed. Bede continued: "By 'religion' the Hindu villager meant *suddha* – living a simple austere life of meditation, often in a degree of solitude. Christians are generally perceived to stand for charitable *organization*, rather than the interior life. What we Western Christians have to learn from the Buddhists and Hindus is their interiority."

Bede believed that wherever they are on the spiritual journey, people are capable of living a contemplative life, a life of surrender and openness, and of living in the present moment. He said: "Contemplation is to see and hear from the heart. It takes us beyond sense perception. It is to relate to things as they are. Contemplative

# Contemplation as a Whole Way of Life

*View from Father Bede's window — a garden dedicated to Saint Romuald*

seeing is not selective, not processed by the brain, nor conditioned by previously held concepts and attitudes. It constitutes a whole way of life . . ."

# Chapter 8
### DRY SEASON, INDIA, 1991-1992
# A New Way of Life – Living from the Centre

*"One could do what was possible by way of showing kindness and talking over difficulties, but ultimately it was prayer alone which prevailed. It is only in prayer that we can communicate with one another at the deepest level of our being. Behind all words and gestures, behind all thoughts and feelings, there is an inner centre of prayer where we can meet one another in the presence of God. It is this inner centre which is the real source of all life and activity and of all love. If we could learn to live from that centre we should be living from the heart of life and our whole being would be moved by love. Here alone can all the conflicts of this life be resolved and we can experience a love which is beyond time and change."*

Bede Griffiths, The Golden String, p. 146

From mid 1990 till mid 1992, I found myself a member of the local Western Australian Inter-Faith Committee, responsible for inviting and raising funds for the proposed visit of His Holiness the XIVth Dalai Lama of Tibet to Australia. This was also expected to be the last opportunity that Father Bede Griffiths would visit our country. Here in Perth, the two men would meet and renew their friendship of many years. They would also engage in serious inter-religious dialogue. While in Australia, Father Bede had the opportunity of meeting many people. He was particularly interested in how men, in particular, found a sense of the spirit in their daily lives. He wanted to know how they fed the hunger for spiritual meaning and purpose in their lives. Bede concluded that Australian men were in a similar position to men in most of the Western world: by and large unsupported in their individual spiritual quests. He found the Churches to be largely ineffectual in their use of language — the use of which no longer spoke in ways that many men could hear and understand. He didn't lay blame at specific doors, but privately he called for a new vision of bringing Christ to modern people, and especially to men. He spoke of the way in which the whole Western world, including the Churches, had been shaped by the masculine developments of the ancient Greek mind, and how there was now a need "to recover the power of the feminine and intuitive mind". He called for the Churches to "turn to the religions of the East, to Hinduism and Buddhism, Taoism, and the subtle blend of all these in Oriental culture, and to the deep intuitions of the tribal cultures of Africa and [Australia], if they are to recover their balance, and evolve an authentic form of religion, which will answer the needs of the modern world".

Father Bede's life was one of gratitude, wonder and awe: he made a difference. Though his life was simple and even austere, he possessed an inner sense of meaning and purpose that radiated and affected all who met him. While deeply concerned at the declining influence of the Church, as far as the inner lives of Western people were concerned, he was nevertheless, the embodiment of someone who is open to, and welcoming of this present moment, the one we each find ourselves in right now.

Bede Griffiths' journey to India was spurred, not so much by the search for new ideas, as for "a new way of life." He found that both the Western culture and church were in some way lacking. It was, he observed again and again, living from the conscious rational level, which is only one half of the soul. His desire was to experience a "marriage of the two dimensions of human existence, the rational and intuitive, the conscious and unconscious, the masculine and feminine." He "wanted to find a way to the marriage of East and West."

When he reached India, Bede became fascinated not with the poverty so much as with the "beauty and vitality" of this new world, and especially of human nature. He wrote: "On all sides was a swarming mass of humanity, children running about quite naked, women in saris, men in turbans, everywhere displaying the beauty of the human form . . . there was grace in all their movements, and I felt that I was in the presence of a hidden power of nature." By contrast, he thought people in the West were "dominated by the conscious mind; they go about their business each shut up in his own ego . . . a fixed determination in their minds, which makes their movements and gestures stiff and awkward, and they all tend to wear the same drab clothes." In spite of the poverty and misery, of which there is enough in India, one of the strongest impressions he had of the country after thirty years was that "in the villages and among the poorest there is an abundance of life and joy."

Bede wrote in his book *The Marriage of East and West* that he went to India to "find the contemplative dimensions of human existence, which the West has almost lost and the East is losing." He was overwhelmed when he visited the Cave of Elephanta near Bombay. Here in the dark and mysterious depths of this immense, multi-pillared cave was a carved image of the Great God *Siva Maheswara*. The impression he had when sighting this colossal image, was of "absolute peace, infinitely distant yet infinitely near, solemn, benign, gentle and majestic. Here, carved in stone, is the very genius of India and the East." This was what Bede had come to India for: the discovery that the Eastern mind is open to both the mind of man and nature "in an intuitive understanding, but also to that hidden Power which pervades both man and nature and reveals to those who are attuned to it the real meaning of human existence."

Throughout India, Bede encountered the concept that every created thing was sacred. He was convinced that this vision of cosmic unity, "in which man and nature are sustained by an all-pervading spirit", this tendency to a more feminine awareness of reality as a whole, is exactly what the West needs to learn from the East. The very earth that is ploughed is sacred, requiring a religious rite before any work commences. Eating is seen as a sacrifice to God. Before taking a wash, the sacred power of the water is invoked. Air, the breath of life, which comes from God, is also sacred, as is fire, which brings light to all creatures. Finally each human being, as a manifestation of God, is also sacred.

Bede Griffiths' occasional visits to the Western world gave him an opportunity to remind his listeners that the universe in which we live has been held to be sacred from the beginning of history. Yet this vision of the universe has been "completely demolished by the Western scientific world." Contemporary humanity finds itself faced with a world in which "every trace of sacredness has been removed from life so that [humanity] finds itself in a universe in which both man and nature have been deprived of ultimate meaning." Even the churches seem "caught up in the present system, and have failed to offer the way of life which people are seeking."

In December of 1990, together with a group of university students from Australia, I travelled to be with Father Bede for his eighty-fourth birthday. Bede welcomed each one and enjoyed their company: their capacity for quietly sitting and listening and for their many questions. I recall him recommending several books for their spiritual reading during their stay at the *ashram*. One of those he suggested was his old friend Donald Nicholl's book, *The Testing of*

*Hearts: A Pilgrim's Journal.* There was Father Bede, sitting in the afternoon-tea rotunda, centred in the middle of the *ashram* compound, sharing a steel cup of very sweet Indian tea among the group of students. Bede had beautiful, long-fingered hands, which seemed to be an extension of his personality. They moved in a slow deliberate way as though in tune with his manner of speaking. He opened

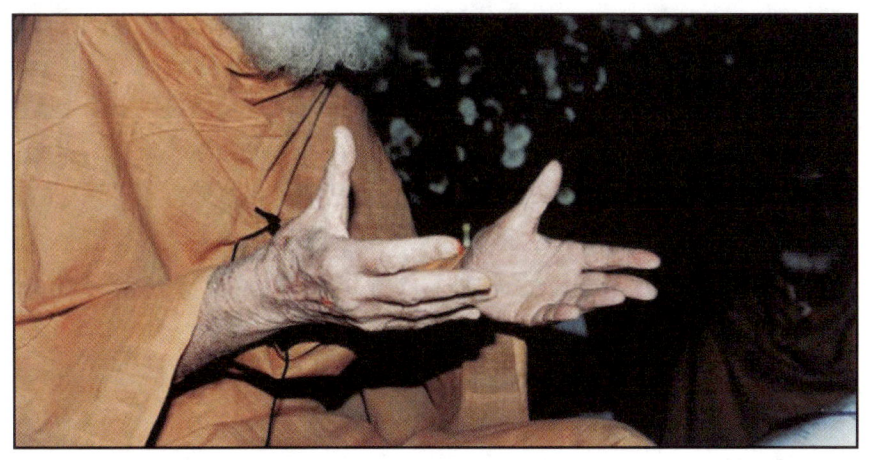

**Father Bede's hands were as eloquent in emphasizing a point as was his voice, 1990**

the pages of Nicholl's book and read everyone a story about two undedicated young men. Their down-to-earth wisdom had a deep significance for Donald Nicholl. The two men had been discussing why it is that men lie to one another. One of them suggested that it's "because they forget about death". He said it seemed to him that there is really only one moment when men recognise the truth. This is when they stand, looking down into the open grave of a friend or relative. But "then they walk away". And within twenty or so yards, "they forget the truth. They begin to lie again". Bede remained silent. Only the sound of ravens calling to each other in the tall palms overhead were heard. Otherwise, all was quiet in the afternoon heat. Then, from the same book, Father Bede read a small Irish prayer for our gathering:

# BEDE GRIFFITHS: FRIEND AND GIFT OF THE SPIRIT

> Three wishes I ask of the King
> when I shall depart from my body:
> may I have nothing to confess,
> may I have no enemy,
> may I have nothing.

What is needed, it seems, is to find a way, a language that helps men and women recover the source of life by returning to their spiritual centre. The outer world, which is studied by science, the world of politics and economics and cultural activity many take for reality. And though important in a way, Bede Griffiths regarded this outer world as "a world of appearances with no reality in itself. It is all passing away at every moment, and everybody is passing with it." Many believe peace will be established on this earth in a kingdom of lasting happiness. But "all this is an illusion . . . the great 'maya' which veils the truth and deceives the world . . . It arises from the refusal to face death." Those who seek fulfilment in this world as an end in itself, see only death. But for those who are willing to die, on a daily basis, to their ego consciousness of the senses and the mind, death is the "breakthrough to a new consciousness . . . and opens on the eternal and the infinite."

But how can men and women, in their everyday activities of life and love, come to know their inner spiritual centre? How can each get to know him or her self? What means are available for ordinary people? Bede's belief was that breaking through to this new consciousness would not happen by more and more thinking. Thinking only reflects one's conscious being. But it will happen through meditation and contemplation, a practice in which each individual will surely confront his dying on a daily basis. He wrote in his book *Return to the Centre* that in meditation we become aware of our solidarity with the universe in all its parts and of the coming into being as well as the passing away of each of those parts. This awareness grows, by way of a journey that takes us "beyond the outer forms of things in time and space" to discover the Ground, from which springs everything that is. The meditator dies to and passes beyond the body and thoughts to find the real Self, which exists in God. Bede tried to explain the end of this journey to the inner spiritual centre, "As a communion of persons in love, in which each understands the other, and is one with the other." In that sense, the individual journey to God is itself the end, the goal. It is already achieved. It is achieved in and by and for Love. He reminds us again: "If we could learn to live from that centre we should be living from the heart of life and our whole being would be moved by love. Here alone can all the conflicts of this life be resolved and we can experience a love which is beyond time and change."

## Chapter 9

AUTUMN, AUSTRALIA, 1992

# Expressing the Inexpressible – the Six Vajra Verses:

*"I felt that I had been wandering in a far country and had returned home; that I had been dead and was alive again; that I had been lost and was found."*

Bede Griffiths, The Golden String, p. 17

In April of 1992, Father Bede, now eighty-six, journeyed to Australia with his companion of many years, Father Christudas. Bede was not well; he arrived frail and tired. While Father Christudas acted as *locum* for my parish in the country, I had arranged for Father Bede to stay with the Australian Sisters of Saint Joseph, south of Perth. Here, in his own apartment, he found rest and quiet, though, as typical of him, he allowed people with personal needs to come and spend time with him privately. My concern was to be free to spend all my time with Bede, attending to his food and rest, and overall schedule of meetings and lectures.

Father Bede chose a way of life that was receptive and open. He valued all religious traditions as well as his own. For him the way of inwardly recognising as yet unimagined possibilities in 'the other' and in how 'the other' sees and describes the truth could lead to a new vision of reality.

The centenary birth of Bede Griffiths occurs in 2006. For over thirty years he lived a life of simplicity and meditation in the *ashram* of the Holy Trinity in Tamil Nadu, South India. In this "Forest of Peace" as it is known to local villagers, Bede not only deepened his personal search "for the other half of [his] soul," but he welcomed spiritual seekers from all over the world, who wished to join him on the inner journey. People of all religions and none found in him the soul of friendship, openness and tolerance: a man of peace, who saw and felt the presence of God in everything and everyone. Bede's own path and the journey that he helped others proceed upon was one of rediscovery. His life was dedicated to a "return to the source of each religious tradition and discover[ing] the basic unity which underlies all religion." Bede lived and taught that beyond the diversity of the universe, there is an inherent unity, or borrowing from modern physicists, "an interdependent network of energies," which ultimately for him was divine love.

As a young man, Bede Griffiths observed the experience of his friends and found he was losing faith in philosophy, reason or the intellect. The poetic imagination, as a way of reflecting on Nature, seemed to be the one anchor-hold in his life to which he continually returned as a means of connecting with reality. He wrote in his autobiography: "The love of nature was the only thing which then moved me deeply, and I found in Wordsworth a religion, which was wholly based on this." As a young man, he could see no connection between the God spoken of in the church and the God who is manifested in Nature. He was drawn to Wordsworth's description of the kind of trance, which he experienced in the presence of Nature, for this came close to his own experience. As he wrote about his yearnings, whether conscious or unconscious, "it was this state of ecstasy which I was seeking all the time . . ." a state in which "I felt that wisdom was to be found, not in philosophy, nor in any form of religion, but in an experience, which gave one a direct insight into the inner meaning of life." Bede Griffiths acknowledged that this was an emotional state and that he sought it continually, though the more he did so, the more it eluded him. He became frustrated and was forced to take another path, "but for many years," he wrote in his autobiography, "this was the inspiration and the goal of my life."

Father Bede commenced his Australian Tour in April-May 1992. The weather was chilly, so I made sure that he was well looked after with a warm room, warm clothes and nourishing food. Though tired after such a long flight, nothing could have dimmed the light in his eyes, a light that was there to the end of his life. It was one of the most disarming things about him. I suspect this may have been one of the sources of attraction for the many people who, through those eyes, sensed the revelation of a heart that was always open and childlike in its desire and readiness to learn something new every day. Let me illustrate how open he was.

On arrival, we walked through my old-fashioned garden of colourful flowers, vinkas and impatiens, violets, palms and marigolds. He loved that garden and would spend some time each day just sitting in contemplation, among flowers, as the breeze rustled through the tall overhanging eucalyptus trees. He also spent a lot of time in my library. As soon as he saw it his face lit up. He exclaimed, "Oh! What a marvellous library. You have all the best and most important books." Straightaway he went to the shelves and began fingering the books and reading their titles. He seemed lost in a world of his own.

**Father Bede in the author's garden, Pinjarra, Western Australia, 1992**

After he'd eaten, he produced from his ever-present hand woven, multicoloured shoulder bag, a small photocopied book, which was stitched together with string. He held it up and said, "I was given this to read recently. It's really one of the most profound books I've ever read." He then carefully turned the first several pages of this now considerably tattered translation by the Tibetan teacher Namkhai Norbu. He read from the Six Vajra Verses:

> Although apparent phenomena
> manifest as diversity
> yet this diversity is non-dual,
> and of all the multiplicity
> of individual things that exist
> none can be confined in a limited concept.
>
> Staying free from the trap of any attempt
> to say it's 'like this', or 'like that',
> it becomes clear that all manifested forms are

aspects of the infinite formless,
and indivisible from it,
are self perfected.

Seeing that everything is self perfected
from the very beginning,
the disease of striving for any achievement
is surrendered,
and just remaining in the natural state
as it is,
the presence of non-dual contemplation
continuously spontaneously arises.

He didn't look up immediately, but when he did, his eyes had a far-away look. He was, I felt, like a child who sees something special and is silenced by awe and wonder.

After a little while, holding the book in his right hand and tapping it with the fingers of his left hand, he said softly, "These are extraordinary words. I have been searching for words to describe this experience of non-dual contemplation all my life. And here it is: the truth of an experience in a few lines!" This experience was deeper than words, definitions and doctrines. Reading and reflecting upon those Six Vajra Verses brought him to a place of understanding that was part of a number of intuitive insights into the nature of the unity of reality that he held towards the end of his life. It seemed to me that the ecstatic experience he had sought since the first glimmer of it in front of the hawthorn bush on that evening at school, was, in his eighty-fifth year, within his grasp — at least that he recognised the possibility of describing the experience of non-duality in the words of others even though they were from another spiritual tradition.

I had heard him speak often, of "wisdom which can transcend reason and know the Truth, not discursively but intuitively, not by its reflection in the world of senses, but in its [ultimate] Ground, where knowing is also being." He taught me that it is this wisdom, which helps us to see that each religious tradition is "a unique revelation of the eternal Truth, the One Word, manifested under particular historical conditions." Truth, which he said is ultimately one, has to be discovered in the heart of each religion "in silence, beyond word and thought." He was certain that if humanity is to survive, it must be through a complete change of heart, so that the conscious mind "may be dethroned and acknowledge its dependence on the Transcendent Mystery."

He sat there lightly tapping that book, looking out the window. Whenever I read those Six Vajra Verses from the Tibetan *Dzogchen* teachings, I think of him and of his remarkable openness to, and his valuing of the wisdom of all of humanity's sacred traditions. Through his discovery of these verses, written in words that are Buddhist symbols of eternal truths, I have become more interested in the depths that I might find in that tradition – not so much to become a Buddhist, but to find a new way of reflecting on the Christian revelation, of Jesus' experience of God as Father, and of Jesus' brotherhood with humanity. The lesson that I've learnt by following Bede Griffiths is that I have never felt impoverished when learning from new perspectives within the faith traditions of others; it has only ever been an enriching experience.

## Chapter 10

### AUTUMN, AUSTRALIA, 1992

# Inter-spiritual Dialogue — A Journey of Surrender

*"And what is sacrifice? To sacrifice is literally to 'make a thing sacred'; it is to take something out of common use and to make it over to God. It is a symbolic act by which we recognise that everything in this world derives from another order of being and seek to enter into communion with that other world. But the outward thing which is sacrificed can never be more than a sign of inward offering; what we desire has to take place in the centre of our own being, in the darkness of the interior where alone we can encounter the God who is hidden in the depths of the soul."*

Bede Griffiths, The Golden String, p. 184

Father Bede's speaking tour of 1992 in Melbourne was significant. In Dallas Brooks Hall alone, he was welcomed by at least 3,000 people who enjoyed listening to him speak of Western Science and Eastern Mysticism. Everywhere he went in Melbourne he was recognised and approached as though a friend of long standing. He listened to everyone, giving as much time as was needed by each. Many felt touched by his extraordinary capacity for self-forgetfulness in their favour.

Together, Father Bede and I made the long journey to the centre of Tibetan teacher and prolific author Geshe Thubten Loden. Here he was received with gracious hospitality and friendliness.

Father Bede acknowledged the individual worth of each person, encouraging them to use their gifts, culture and faith for the good of their community. He gave himself to that Love which lies at the heart of human existence and shapes our lives. But, he said, "It is a love which reveals itself in an agony of self-surrender on the Cross, and makes itself known to those who are prepared to make the same surrender."

The Venerable Acharya Geshe Loden is the Tibetan teacher

Father Bede, Tibetan Ven Geshe Loden Acharya, and the author, Melbourne, Australia, 1992

of a spiritual community outside of Melbourne. He welcomed Fr. Bede and me to his centre as though greeting old friends. Bede sought information about the teachings of *Dzogchen*. Interfaith dialogue is extremely difficult, slow, and sometimes not very productive when those involved do not speak each other's language. Just such problems dogged Bede and Geshe Loden during their afternoon of sharing. However, much more was communicated between these two men than mere propositions about each other's philosophical or spiritual traditions and doctrines.

Bede Griffiths' understanding of Tibetan *Dzogchen* meditation had matured and ripened since his discovery of Namkhai Norbu's treatise on the Six Vajra Verses. He brought this ripened thinking with him to his meeting with Geshe Loden in Melbourne. Bede's discovery of the Tibetan view of non-duality was valuable for him as a way of clarifying the depths of his Christian faith. Particularly in his later years, Bede came to see the importance of meditation for Christians. Deeply affected by the sufferings of the Tibetan people, he asked Geshe Loden if he and the Tibetan people found meditation helpful during the years of repression under the Red Army's occupation. Geshe Loden responded:

> Since 1959, and in spite of the Red Army's bombs, destruction and killings, meditation has been vital in helping Tibetan people see that in some way, their own karma brought the Chinese into Tibet. In some way our karma is involved in the Chinese attitude to the Tibetan people. Chinese people do not normally want to kill others, so they are also living out their karma in relation to the Tibetan people. Yes, meditation is extremely important. It helps us develop a more compassionate attitude, which is helpful, because in fact, the Chinese and we Tibetans are not two, but one. The whole universe is included in the concept of non-duality. While there are distinctions between things, all are included in the oneness. Therefore non-duality thinking is most important, for it destroys negative thinking.

Geshe Loden and Father Bede went on to discuss the different systems of Tibetan meditation. *Dzogchen*, meaning 'Great Perfection,' claimed Bede's keen attention. The Tibetans regard it as a means of realisation and of experiencing the fullness of wisdom and compassion. He felt there were striking similarities between this system and Christianity. He said: "In *Dzogchen*, the primordial state, the supreme reality, where everything is contained in perfect wholeness, fullness and bliss, is realised suddenly, without the need for preparatory steps of *yoga* and meditation training." Likewise, for Bede, in the Christian tradition, contemplation is a gift, a 'grace' from God. It is not something individuals acquire through meditation, or any other personal exertion. It comes to those who are ready to receive it, as God's action in us, rather than the result of our own effort. In Bede's understanding, Buddhism sees the supreme reality as a gift of awakening transmitted to the disciple by his *guru*. In Christianity, Bede taught, this realisation comes "as a gift of the Spirit through Christ, the *Sat-Guru*, the supreme teacher who communicates his inner life to his disciples."

As far as Bede understood *Dzogchen*, new students moved from the basic stage of training called *sutra* — following the meditation teaching of the Buddha by way of doctrine and discipline such as *yoga* and other complex rituals. The next stage, called *Tantra* — focuses on the body: the breath, the blood, the five senses and feelings. It is in this practice that the individual draws on the powers of the unconscious. As far as Bede could determine, many Christians are ignorant of the unconscious realm, having, by and large, been brought up to concentrate on the conscious level. He believed that Christians need to recover a sense of the unconscious, where the human being is one with the dynamic forces of nature. It is the task of *Tantra*, he asserted, to open the individual to these powerful unconscious forces, which after appropriate training, may in various ways be controlled or at least brought under the dominion of higher consciousness.

There is a third stage in *Dzogchen* practice called the Primordial State. This, Bede reflected, exists from the beginning, hidden behind the body, the feelings, the senses, and all limitations. Through *Dzogchen*, the practitioner realises the Buddha nature within, thus entering into Buddha-hood. The aim of this practice is to become open to the infinite and the eternal, which is in everyone and everything throughout the cosmos. In his observation, many Westerners typically live and practice religion in the body and psyche though had not yet discovered the spirit. As a consequence, he observed that Western religion tended to be all in the conscious mind, the will, which doubtless is good as far as it goes. But for Bede, beyond the body and psyche is the realm of the *pneuma*, the spirit, what Saint Francis de Sales calls the 'fine point of the soul,' and theologian Karl Rahner refers to as the point of self-transcendence.

Bede Griffiths warned that meditators could sometimes become so absorbed in concentrating the mind that the world is "lost". Under these circumstances, relating to the world becomes difficult, sometimes viewing it as an illusion, which he says, "is a sort of dualism." *Dzogchen* can teach Christians the necessity of "integrating all levels of reality in the supreme wisdom." In Buddhism this is called *prajna*. In Christianity it is called *gnosis*, or Divine Knowledge. Buddhists understand the Primordial State as total oneness: everything gathered into unity, and then manifesting itself in the multiplicity of the universe: earth, sky, nature, and people, all manifestations of the supreme wisdom reflected as in a mirror, a mirror of the primordial state. The idea of reaching such total oneness is very close, said Father Bede, to the Christian idea of *pleroma*, fullness. However, the idea that Christ is the one in whom the fullness of Divine Reality is totally present has not the same implication for Buddhists. In his later years, Father Bede realised that he needed to exercise a degree of prudence when drawing too firm a conclusion as to how Buddhist and Christian mysticism were aligned. Ultimately, the fullness of Divine Reality, whether understood according to the insights of Buddhism or Christianity, was beyond thought, and beyond words.

Words can get in the way of dialogue, though in the service of better dialogue there is a need for technical clarity on both sides. Bede

**View of the community rotunda, Saccidananda ashram**

Griffiths spent much of his life seeking appropriate words for the wisdom that he felt all round him. Each day he sought ways of communicating that wisdom more effectively to seekers who gathered round him at *Shantivanam*. Bede was true to his insights and his faith. While opening more and more to the religions of the world, he would return to his faith foundations. He reminded his listeners: "for Christians then, the Father is the source, the origin, the one beyond, who can't be named properly. The name Father is only a name for that which is beyond all name and form, yet the Father, the source, manifests himself in the Word, Jesus."

At the end of the day we parted from the centre as we came, as welcome guests and friends. Geshe Loden graciously invited us to return whenever we could and stay longer. Father Bede could sit in dialogue among teachers of all spiritual traditions and listen with respect to what they had to share. This he did while also respectfully and humbly communicating his own understanding of spiritual truths and the Christian community to which he had given his life.

# Chapter 11
## AUTUMN, AUSTRALIA, 1992
# Two Elders Meet Across the Traditions

*"Modern physics itself is changing our idea of the structure of the universe . . . [the] physical world cannot be separated from the psyche, from the consciousness . . . We have a physical world and a psychic world which are interrelated and interdependent . . . Mankind has been changed because mankind is ultimately one, an organic, interdependent whole extending through space and time."*

Bede Griffiths, *The Cosmic Revelation, pp. 20 & 128.*

Father Bede was open to the beauty and truth that existed particularly in indigenous cultures. He saw the ancestral myths and rituals and the dance and song of the Aboriginal people of Australia, as with tribal people everywhere, as ways of setting humanity free from its isolation and restoring original unity with itself and the universe. The insights into ultimate reality contained in these cultures, he said, are called the Cosmic Covenant. This is the revelation of ultimate truth, given to all mankind through the cosmos. In this regard, Bede refers to Paul's Letter to the Romans: "Ever since the creation of the world, his invisible nature, namely his eternal power and divinity has been clearly perceived in the things that are made." Bede suggests that beyond historical structures, Christianity too has its original myths. These need to be recovered, he postulated, but it cannot be done by the Western mind alone. "We have", says Bede, "to open ourselves to the revelation of the divine mystery", evidence of which intuitive wisdom is left all over the world, among such cultures as the Australian Aboriginals. This, Bede said, is because the divine Mystery, the ultimate Truth, "always lies beyond our conception." Yet, each in its own way reveals different aspects of the Mystery "according to the imaginative insight of the different people of the world."

Thus Bede had profound respect for the Aboriginal people of Australia, and had expressed the desire to meet with local Aboriginals if possible. When he met with Elder Gaboo of the Wallaga Lake people at the Benedictine Monastery in Sydney, he felt that judging by the space they made for each other's spiritualities, he'd met his brother and kindred spirit on common ground. He felt that between them was the bond of infinite communion.

Father Bede and Elder Gaboo, Saint Benedict's Monastery, New South Wales, 1992

## Two Elders Meet Across the Traditions

Sixty thousand years before European colonisation of the Australian continent, the Aboriginal inhabitants had developed their own mystical spirituality. Theirs was a spirituality that embraced oneness with the land and all its creatures. Aboriginal people considered the total environment as living, conscious, and connected with every other part. *'Dadirri'* has a special meaning for Aboriginal Australians. Aboriginal Elder Miriam-Rose Ungunmerr describes the word *'dadirri'* of the Australian Aboriginal Ngangikurungkurr Tribe (from the Daly River in far northern Australia) as "a kind of contemplation, engaged in the bush, campfire setting or ceremony, and combining 'inner deep listening and quiet still awareness . . . and waiting.'" This attitude of mind, when culturally reinforced, must, it would seem, be a rich source of experience and understanding of relationships with others and spirituality in daily life. Australian priest and contemporary commentator on multi-culturalism Eugene Stockton questions whether this word and its meaning might in some way extend into the spiritual-cultural life of the country, showing the way to an Australian mysticism that "seeks the Transcendent Other, immanent in the environment."

In 1992 the Wallaga Lake people of New South Wales made contact with me, asking if the Elder Gaboo of their tribe might come and meet with Father Bede. Bede and I were staying, as guests, at Saint Benedict's Monastery in Arcadia, not far from Sydney. I sent word that Elder Gaboo would be most welcome to come and sit with Bede. When these two senior men, both with long white beards and flowing hair, met, it was like a meeting of old friends, or of two brothers. They held each other in a warm embrace and looked at each other. I felt the silence said everything that needed to be said between them. It was a true *'dadirri'* experience of "inner deep listening and quiet still awareness."

Bede spoke with Elder Gaboo of his simple life at the *ashram* in India. With a sparkle in his voice he said: "I have this little hermitage now, at the *ashram*. It's in the forest, some distance from the main buildings. Here, I can go away and spend time by myself in silence and solitude. I feel I have absolute simplicity here. You know, I learn so much when I live this simple life." He described his admiration for the simplicity of Aboriginal people and felt that they have much to teach other Australians and the world. Father Bede had always sympathised with traditional societies, though in many ways, he recognised that he was 'out of step' with the modern world's value on this matter. His feeling was that as long as the predominantly European cultures tried to "fit the people of indigenous cultures into their scheme of things, dialogue and mutual respect would never be achieved."

Father Bede had prepared for this meeting by reading some of the works of Father Eugene Stockton by which he was fascinated. Stockton's archaeological research of Aboriginal history and his contribution toward a genuinely 'Australian spirituality' were much admired by Bede. He became aware of the ways in which indigenous Australians might contribute to greater awareness of how the stories of The Dreamtime honoured and celebrated all of creation and taught laws that allowed for the continuation of each species of life on earth. He was reminded of the way indigenous people had a world view that was more 'family' based than hierarchical, more diffuse than linear and clear, as it tended to be in Western European thinking. Immersed as he was in the idea of universal inter-relatedness, he saw how, for indigenous people, every part of the land, the whole earth and entire cosmos was sacred. He reviewed his understanding of how the people have a special kinship that regarded stewardship, not exploitation, as a basic and permanent social value. Underlying these perspectives, Bede realised that Aboriginal Australians had a profound desire to live in harmony with the land and with all living things. For Aboriginals, each part of the cosmos had its own laws, but each respected the autonomy of every other

## Two Elders Meet Across the Traditions

part, in a way that enabled the people to conform individual life to the pattern and balance set by tradition. Bede knew how Aboriginal culture had suffered for the last two centuries, but he was inspired by the way these people accepted life as a mixture of good and bad. This was an attitude that could, if practised wisely, lead to contentment and simplicity. Indigenous people, he understood, had an approach to time that came from The Dreamtime, where past and future are contained in the now. Deadlines simply have no meaning for Aboriginal people. Thus, there is a priority of persons over things, and of exploring relationships, rather than of asking what one does for work. Having such an attitude disposes the Aboriginal person to hospitality and sharing, an attitude that confuses and sometimes angers other Australians. But over all, Bede realised that among Aboriginal Australians there is a profound sense of creative accommodation to adversity, a sense of good humour, an attitude of not taking oneself too seriously, and a sense of celebration. Of course Bede was practical, and he understood that the non-Aboriginal Australian community would need to take time to fully understand and embrace the values as expressed in Stockton's research. But he did believe that every Australian could do well to consider the spiritual depth of these values and try, in whatever individual way possible, to incorporate them into personal daily contemplative practice.

When Elder Gaboo met Bede he explained to him how he travels the world speaking of Aboriginal spirituality. He expressed his sadness at how his people had become so reduced, "going from bad to worse." Though he added: "Yet you know my brother, love will overcome." To which Bede said: "Yes my friend, love is the meaning of life."

Bede believed that paramount cultures tend to want to eliminate simple cultures, as had happened so tragically in Australia. But he added that ultimately, a "renewal would take place". Bede foresaw there "would be a rebirth of the good" that lies within the ancient indigenous cultures of the world. These cultures have a deep sense of spirituality, and a profound connection with Nature and the whole earth that will help save the world. He expressed his optimism and confidence: "we are slowly recovering the sense of respect for the earth and the creatures of the earth", and this was the necessary understanding the world needed at this time. It is knowledge that is based on making space for listening to and learning from other traditions in the service of humanity as well as of the planet.

Bede exchanged views with the Elder as to how the indigenous religions view God, not as "up there" and "above," but as "present in the earth and air and water." He illustrated his understanding with a story about his predecessor at the *ashram* Father Jules Monchanin, who went up to a group of school children and asked: "Where is God?" Some of the children were Christians, and they all pointed skywards saying: "God is in heaven." But all the Hindu children pointed to their breasts: "God is in the heart."

Bede was interested in learning about Aboriginal rituals because he realized that educating people about these rituals was critical to the survival of indigenous religions. In particular he wanted to know about the Elder's custom of going to a mountainous place to meditate. The Elder said that when he was not able to go to a mountain, he would meditate wherever he found himself. Each day he would "thank the Great Spirit, morning and night, for his life." He said: "That's the place you've got to go brother. To the mountain." There was a little silence as Bede looked at his friend. Elder Gaboo, tapping his breast, said: "The place of the mountain is here, within, in the heart."

Elder Gaboo also expressed how he "believed that Australia is the Promised Land." He explained that once upon a time "there was a great man who came and sat on a log with the people, who all came to be with him. He ate all the things that the local people ate - goanna and wallaby, and so on . . . He shared everything with the people, and they listened to everything he said. After a while . . . you know brother, that in The Dreamtime, a while could mean a long time . . . the great man said: 'I'm going now, but I will come again.' He then pointed to the East and said: 'That is where I'm coming from.' His name is Garama." Bede and I weren't sure what this meant, but it was an interesting and provocative insight into an aspect of Elder Gaboo's spirituality. He spoke in a way that came, we felt, from 'Dreamtime language', beyond rational interpretation, in the face of which, very little could be interpreted or presumed.

Elder Gaboo and Father Bede sat in a small monastic interview room. I was there recording the dialogue and serving tea. Bede said that he believed everyone has to recognise the unique value of his or her own religion. Having done this, they can then relate it to other religions with their claims of salvation, offers of freedom from suffering in this world, and rewards of everlasting life or liberation. He pointed out that "until recently, Christianity customarily dismissed all other religions as false. But from their point of view, some other religions have the same attitude", he said. Nevertheless, he urged, "This attitude is something religions have to overcome." Bede believed that individuals must regard his or her "own religion in its relation to other religions," so as to find that "which is unique and of value in each." This, he argued, "is the spiritual way of the future: making space for the other in mature dialogue, learning from each other, and being of service to each other."

At the end of the visit, Elder Gaboo became silent. After a while he said: "When I saw you were here in Australia I thought it was marvellous! I felt I wanted to come out here and see you. I'm happy that I have come. When I looked at you, I realised I already knew you. I'm speaking from the Dreamtime you know." There was a pause. The two men held each other's gaze. After a little while, Bede responded very gently and appreciatively. He said: "We are kindred spirits." Another pause. Elder Gaboo responded: "Yes we are

Elder Gaboo and Father Bede in dialogue,
Saint Benedict's Monastery, New South Wales, 1992

brother." Silence. Then, without any signal, we all rose. The two men, Gaboo and Bede, drew close and warmly embraced each other. Bede later said he knew he would never again see his new friend. There were tears in his eyes as the Elder departed to his waiting car. Bede had received two carved and decorated traditional message sticks, as gifts from Elder Gaboo. He held them tenderly and looked down at them. I allowed the silence to linger and did not say a word. That evening after supper Bede said that in this meeting, he experienced one of the most meaningful connections of his life. I felt it to have been a genuine experience of '*dadirri*', where all of us enjoyed a time of contemplative inner deep listening, quiet still awareness . . . and respectful waiting. We could have been sitting under a mallee tree in the bush, in a campfire setting or a simple ceremony of friendship and exchanging of gifts, the most precious being perception of mutual respect.

# Chapter 12
## AUTUMN, AUSTRALIA, 1992
# Appreciating the Greatness in Others

*"The divine life penetrates history, time, suffering, and death, and then raises [them] into a new creation, a new order of being in which these things are not lost, not destroyed, but transfigured. This gives a value to every human person."*

Bede Griffiths, The Cosmic Revelation, p. 127

In April and May of 1992, His Holiness the Dalai Lama of Tibet and Father Bede Griffiths both arrived in Australia for their respective national lecture tours. As part of an interfaith committee, and over a period of time, we had raised funds to support His Holiness' tour in every necessary way. Approximately 20,000 people came to sit in the presence of the Dalai Lama at his two ceremonies in Perth. Father Bede was one of them. His Holiness made a deliberate exit from his entrance procession to make straight for Father Bede and embrace him with great joy, warmth and reverence.

In the same week, the Western Australian capital city of Perth hosted both His Holiness the XIVth Dalai Lama and Bede Griffiths. I was fortunate to have been involved in the invitations sent to these teachers, as well as the fund-raising activities to provide airfares and accommodation throughout their journeys.

Prior to the public lectures arranged for His Holiness, there was a meeting between him and Bede. It had been some years since last they met. The Dalai Lama came straight up to Father Bede, took him by the shoulders, smiled and gazed into his eyes. Then all of a sudden, His Holiness played the fingers of both his hands through Bede's long white beard. Evidently amazed at this display of affection, I remember Bede's eyes nearly popped. Quickly recovering, a wide smile spread across his face. This delighted His Holiness, who once again embraced him, laughing loudly and playfully in his familiar manner.

This was a significant gathering, for here present were His Holiness' assistants from Dharamsala, namely Tenzin Geshe Tethong and the Venerable Lobsang Jordhen, his Religious Affairs Adviser, but also the senior lamas who had over the years come to Australia to establish meditation centres throughout the country. It seems everyone had gathered in Perth for this historic event.

Almost immediately, before the gathering had time to formally commence, Father Bede turned to the Dalai Lama and asked him: "I wonder if Your Holiness would explain something about *Dzogchen* meditation. It is a practice in which I have become very interested in recent times." From their reactions I could see the surrounding lamas were completely surprised that Father Bede had asked this question, or that he knew about this specialised and relatively unknown contemplative practice. From the conversation that followed between the two men, I felt the respect for Father Bede grew visibly among the assembled college of Tibetan lamas.

At the end of the evening, two senior lamas approached Bede and bowed quite low. One, the elder of the two, while taking Bede's hand in both of his, said with measured emphasis: "Father, you are a very great man." I felt as though I was witness to a moment of profound connection between masters of two quite different traditions.

# Chapter 13
## AUTUMN, AUSTRALIA, 1992
# God and the Universe are Not Two

*"... there is nothing which is not holy. The simplest actions of eating and drinking, of washing and cleaning, of walking and sitting ... have a sacramental character; they signify something beyond themselves and are intimately related to religious rites. So also every form of work ... is part of a sacramental mystery, by which we enter into communion with the rhythm of nature and take part in that ritual by which the life of man is continually renewed."*

Bede Griffiths, *The Golden String* p. 152

For Bede Griffiths, the difference between the Semitic religions — Judaism, Christianity and Islam — and the Oriental religions of Hinduism, Buddhism and Taoism, seemed to lie in this; that in the Semitic tradition, God is represented as the transcendent Lord of creation, infinitely 'holy', that is, separate from and above nature and never to be confused with it. However, in the Oriental tradition, God, or the Absolute, is immanent in all creation. The world does not exist apart from God, but 'in' God; God dwells in the heart of everything.

Now, while this has certain shortcomings, as far as Bede could determine, it is a view that he believed Christianity could learn much from.

In his spiritual direction of others, or during his homilies, Father Bede referred to the wisdom teachings of the early Church. One of his observations was that for many Christians, basing their thinking on the biblical thought and language used in relation to educating children in the faith, God remains a 'person'. Such language is limited, yet Christians are hardly aware of these limits. Bede preferred to return to such thinkers as Dionysius the Areopagite, who, under the influence of the Neo-Platonists, described God as 'beyond being'. He encouraged learning also from the Oriental traditions that describe the Godhead as *Brahman, Atman*, or the Tao, or in the extreme negative language of Buddhism – Nirvana or the Void. Whatever the word used, they all point towards the nameless reality, which cannot be properly conceived, and is as much beyond personality as it is beyond human concept. This knowledge, found in Buddhism and Christianity alike, at its deepest level, is recognised as knowledge above reason, a knowledge that is not derived from the senses and is not determined by the categories of rational thought. His consistent exhortation was that Christian churches have to turn to the religions of the East, to Hinduism, Buddhism and Taoism if they are to recover their balance and evolve an authentic form of religion, which is capable of answering the needs of the modern world.

On the last day of the Dalai Lama's 1992 visit to Perth, I received a phone call from his private secretary, Tenzin Geshe Tethong. He invited Bede Griffiths and myself to a private audience with His Holiness before he left for other capitals. What was meant to be a short courtesy visit lasted ninety minutes. Following an exchange of warm greetings, Bede and I sat in the three-seater lounge. His Holiness occupied a single armchair nearby. The atmosphere was extremely friendly and relaxed. Almost immediately, the conversation turned to the mystery of God. His Holiness was genuinely interested

**His Holiness the Dalai Lama, Tenzin Yeshe Tethong, Father Bede and the author, Perth, Western Australia, 1992**

in how Christians conceptualised and spoke of God and God's nature. In later discussions, both Bede and I opined that His Holiness displayed an intuitive perception of Christianity, despite his lack of exposure to it.

In the course of the morning, Father Bede spoke of the way Christianity inherited the typically Hebrew understanding of God, as a Being of utter transcendence; a holy mystery that no one could approach; a Being of absolute moral perfection and justice, and yet of infinite mercy. He followed this point, showing that by the time of the New Testament, God is spoken of in intimate relation to humankind. But generally speaking, he said, it is not until the times of the Greek Fathers that there is a development of the understanding of the divine nature. His Holiness seemed fascinated when Bede quoted Saint Clement of Alexandria: "The deity is without form and nameless. Though we ascribe names, they are not to be taken in their strict meaning. When we call him one, good, mind, existence, Father, God, Creator, Lord . . . we use these [names] of honour in order that our thought may have something to rest on."

One of the points that came up in the dialogue was His Holiness' notion that Christians believe in the idea of "God out there," of a God that is separate from the universe. In response, Bede pointed out that according to traditional Christianity, "God and the universe are not two." He went on to say that the typically Western notion of God as separate from nature, that is, standing against the universe, is an idea that is no longer valid today, though many people still hang on to that approach. Consistent with his earlier assertions, he gently said:

> Thanks to modern science and dialogue between religions, we now understand that the universe exists in relation to the transcendent reality as a whole. So, today it is important to understand that God and the universe are not dual, not two. Neither are they one. So, in terms of the universe and God, we cannot speak of pantheism. Instead I speak of the way of relationship: that is, the universe exists simply in relationship to the transcendent whole.

He made the point several times, as he felt it to be extremely important for the modern world. This view is also of tremendous importance in interfaith dialogue where East is meeting West, and science is meeting mysticism. Father Bede referred to the theologian Thomas Aquinas, pointing out that he would agree with this understanding. Aquinas' teaching had close affinity with the teachings of the early Hindu teacher of *Advaita* Shankara-Acharya. In concluding this aspect of the conversation, Father Bede said:

> The universe of multiplicity of things, of coming into being, and of constant change, has no being in itself: it exists in relation to the one transcendent whole. That view is acceptable to the traditional Christian view when properly understood. Many

Christians are fixed in the dualistic approach, and are afraid to go beyond that. But I feel that we are moving from this Aristotelian dualistic view of the universe, to a more non-dualistic view point: that is, the whole universe is based in non-dual relationship to the transcendent whole, which is common to Christianity, Islamic Sufism and the Hindu-Buddhist traditions.

We were concerned that we might have overstayed our allotted time. We need not have worried. His Holiness was fascinated. His interest was piqued again when Bede talked of the sixth century monk, who wrote under the name of Dionysius the Areopagite. For the first time, Bede said, we find the whole problem of the nature of God and human understanding of this mystery, to be systematically worked out. Dionysius held that God is utterly incomprehensible and could only be known in ecstasy, when the mind passes beyond itself, transcending speech and thought. Indeed, his doctrine included the notion that God is as much above all being as above all thought, "above everything that exists." For Dionysius, the Godhead is beyond being itself. In this sense, he described Dionysius' teaching as similar to that of the Indian mystic Nagarjuna, who taught a way of systematically eliminating all names, concepts and images in reference to the Godhead. Bede developed the thought of passing beyond every thought and every existing thing, so as to reach the supreme Godhead. Yet, he said, "all energy, all life, all consciousness, reason and will comes from this source, and are therefore, in some way, contained in it." To attain knowledge of the supreme Godhead, we must pass, he said, beyond all images and concepts, into a kind of 'unknowing,' where we leave behind human notions of god-like things, thus leaving ourselves open to receiving the 'ray of divine darkness'. We realise the limitations of, and therefore go beyond the human means of expressing the divine nature. To even attempt to describe what is happening, Father Bede acknowledged, language in such matters has to be mystical language — a way of comprehending and articulating that proposes: "God is experienced in the darkness, as light beyond the darkness, and as light in the darkness".

His Holiness had thought that Christians insisted that their words were permanent and definitive explanations of the mysteries. He had, it seemed to me, been encouraged and reassured during this morning's conversation. He was clearly interested in what Father Bede said: "In the abyss of the Godhead, that divine darkness, there is a mystery of personal communion, in which all that we can conceive of as wisdom and knowledge, love and bliss, is contained, yet which infinitely transcends our conception . . . [for] the Godhead remains unfathomable, transcending human thought."

Accepting that His Holiness was happy to afford the time, Father Bede continued. He quoted from the works of Dionysius, who counselled his readers to suspend their senses and intellectual activity. Once the rational understanding was laid to rest, the individual may strive toward a union with him whom no human understanding can contain: "for by the unceasing and absolute renunciation of yourself and all things . . . you shall be released from all, and so be led upwards to the Ray of that divine darkness, which exceeds all existence." There were many aspects of Christianity shared that morning, but Bede consistently returned to the doctrine of Dionysius and the Fathers of the Church.

At this stage, His Holiness left his armchair and joined us on the lounge. He held Father Bede's hand. While looking him in the eye, he said: "You know Father, I never knew Christians could think like this." It was, I felt, a deeply moving moment. We remained sitting companionably together for the rest of the morning. I found the Dalai Lama's interest in everything Bede said to be sincere and engaged. Towards the end of our visit, Bede remarked: "Your Holiness, as sad and painful as the history of the Tibetan *Diaspora* has

The Dalai Lama, Fr. Bede and the author, Perth, Western Australia, 1992

been, it may very well be the means whereby Western people will take up meditation and recover their own contemplative riches." His Holiness was fascinated and readily agreed. He restated his oft-repeated belief that, for him, there will never be one world religion for everyone. He avowed that there is goodness and truth to be found in all spiritualities of the world, but in the meantime, he hoped that Western people everywhere, would be able to at least learn meditation from teachers of the Tibetan tradition.

When we finally departed His Holiness' presence, we were both elated and pensive. I thanked Bede for his teaching. I noted that His Holiness had the opportunity of clarifying his understanding of Christianity. During the morning interview, I believe Father Bede had given of himself, as whole-heartedly as in any of his larger lectures when he spoke to thousands. I recall one of the nicest touches at the end of this unique and inspiring experience. Bede took me by the elbow as we walked from the audience. He spoke of his meeting with the Dalai Lama, and remarked with considerable emotion and with a tear in his eye: "You know, I really do think he likes me!"

# Chapter 14
AUTUMN, AUSTRALIA, 1992
# Meditation – Some Practical Guidance

*". . . in meditation the mind keeps wandering. We keep bringing it back, and it wanders again and we bring it back again; and so it goes on, maybe for months and years, until at last the mind becomes stabilised . . . thoughts go roving around in the head, but if we bring them down into the heart, that is, the centre of the person, there they come to rest."*

Bede Griffiths, *River of Compassion:*
*A Christian Commentary on the Bhagavad Gita, p. 122*

This memoir is taken from a talk that touched on various aspects of meditation as practised at *Shantivanam*. It is a general guide to the overall understanding and teaching of meditation for Father Bede, who said: "Contemplation is to see and hear from the heart. It takes us beyond sense perception. It is to relate to things as they are. Contemplative seeing is not selective. It is not processed by the brain nor conditioned by previously held concepts and attitudes. It constitutes a whole way of life . . ."

In the lush green mountain valleys of Victoria, not far from Melbourne, Dr Ian Gawler and his wife have built a beautiful rural

# BEDE GRIFFITHS: FRIEND AND GIFT OF THE SPIRIT

**Father Bede and Dr Ian Gawler, Yarra Glen, Victoria, Australia, 1992**

retreat centre for people suffering from cancer. Here in an atmosphere of great beauty, patients learn meditation under Ian's guidance. He himself suffered cancer which resulted in the amputation of his leg many years ago. It was, in part, through meditation that he battled his way back to health. Father Bede and Ian had met at *Shantivanam* in 1988. Father Bede had read and liked Ian's books. He asked me to take him to visit the Gawlers, where he was asked to address patients and staff on the subject of meditation.

Father Bede divulged how essential meditation is in the lives of the community at *Shantivanam*. Before he described the techniques of meditation in any depth, he stressed the importance of becoming people of inner and outer peace. He described the process of helping the body to relax, of bringing the body to a point of complete stillness and peace. He emphasized too, that breathing is important. Breath is the mediator between the body and the mind he said, for example, when the mind becomes disturbed, the breathing also becomes agitated. Father Bede spoke of his late friend Swami Amaldas, whom he said was a great teacher of *yoga* at the *ashram*. He told how Amaldas taught visitors to breathe in with the sacred word

'*Jesu*', and breathe out with the sacred word 'Abba.' The repetitive use of a sacred word or sound is an ancient practice in India called *Nama japa*. Bede pointed out to his listeners that it goes back at least as far as Patanjali, who said in his *yoga sutras* that *yoga*, the way of union with God, is "the cessation of the movements of the mind." He recommended sitting and quietly repeating the mantra or sacred word. "Of course", he said, "the mind will wander off. When one realises this, one gently comes back to the sacred word". He assured the gathering that this is "a process that may last for hours. Though at the *ashram* our meditation periods are usually much shorter." He said this last statement with humour and a twinkle in his eye. Father Bede never made a show of great achievements in the spiritual life. He was modest and regarded the *ashram* as a place where ordinary people tried their best to do what they could. He was careful not to allow people to become worried if they did not measure up to standards they may have heard or read about.

Late afternoon sun gleamed through the large windows. It seemed to me that all his listeners were deeply interested. He spoke about becoming still and calm, so as to be "more aware of the deeper levels of consciousness." Raising his hand for emphasis, he said:

> Otherwise, one remains imprisoned in the merely rational mind. Look at the way we educate children today. They begin, so early, to develop their rational minds. Indeed, I learnt French when I was four, and Latin when I was seven, and Greek when I was nine, until I almost had a breakdown. Of course, it was then that something deeper had the possibility of emerging.

Without becoming too technical, Bede made reference to the threefold nature of the human being as body, soul, and spirit. He asserted that to get beyond the mind is the great problem. In a way, he said, it is the mind that controls the body. Many diseases of the body are the product of stress and anxiety in the mind. His audience could understand this. Several nodded their heads in agreement as he continued: "Healing takes place in the deeper self, beyond the mind. It is here that one becomes aware of a healing power, the spirit, the divine healer that is within everybody." To explain this more deeply and clearly, he sat closer to the edge of his seat and went on:

> The body is the physical organism, and our link with the whole of nature. The *psyche*, or soul, is the psychological organism with its hopes and thoughts, feelings, anxieties and disturbances. But beyond this is the *pneuma* – in India called the *atman*, the deep Self where one transcends the ego. It is the 'place,' if you like, of union with the transcendent, the spirit, [and the] higher self.

After thirty years in the *ashram*, Bede understood and had personally integrated the finer points of Indian mysticism. He felt it desirable to share some elements of this with his Australian listeners. He said: "This deep peace, beyond name or form that is aimed at and experienced in profound meditation, is called 'saccidananda,' being, consciousness, and bliss." Once again, he acknowledged that each person is at a different stage on the path. He reminded us that it is a matter of taking small steps first, but eventually those steps will lead to that deep centre beyond the mind. Once that happens, he pointed out, once we get beyond the separate ego, we have the opportunity of "coming to that place of deep happiness, wisdom and rest, called the deep Self." Describing the reality of the human condition, he declared that from birth, everyone is self-centred. It is natural and necessary. "But eventually," he stressed, "one has to get beyond that separate self, to Love, to the transcendent whole. It is divine Love that breaks through the ego. Let go of the ego, and your life is transformed. But it requires letting go, surrender; a kind of death really."

Presuming that most of his audience was Christian, Bede spoke of the many Westerners who visit the *ashram* seeking peace of mind, yet who are often overwhelmed by mental turmoil. With deep concern he asserted that often from childhood they had been taught to suppress negative feelings such as anger, fear, hatred and desire, and ill advisedly they have pushed these negative feelings down deep in their unconscious. He sounded a cautionary note that the more one represses these feelings, the more powerful and negative they become. He made the point strongly: "Feelings should never be repressed, but allowed into the consciousness. In my experience, many Christians are plagued by feelings of sin, guilt and fear because of the training they have received. No feeling is so bad that it can't be changed to a positive direction if allowed into the open consciousness." Having given spiritual direction to *ashram* visitors for decades, he was clear when he made the point that it is vital for someone on the spiritual journey to open up the ordinary, personal consciousness to the deep Self, the transcendent spirit, the higher self where, as he said: "Love may be found and where Love may heal." Drawing the gathering to a close, he shared something quite powerful of his personal experience in the recent past:

> Let me explain what I mean. I had the experience of a stroke in 1989. I was completely laid out and couldn't speak or walk for over a week. But as I came round, I found my ego, my mental consciousness, had been knocked down. It was as though I had a blow on the head. It was an extraordinary experience. My ego consciousness was eradicated, and, as the deeper self began to emerge, I saw everything embraced as a unity, as a harmony, instead of disunity and divided. I feel it was the opening of the deep Self, of Love. I was completely overwhelmed by this Love.

Bede then laughingly shared with his listeners: "I am advising people to have a stroke! Though of course there is a gentler way of doing it than that." As if to reinforce the point he had just made, his voice softened, he leaned forward and said with great sensitivity:

> But quite honestly I believe that any serious accident, disease, or loss in life can be a means of breakthrough. One lives in one's world in the family and at work in personal consciousness. Everything seems happy enough. But then, suddenly one is overtaken by tragedy, which can be a means of transformation. Everything seems appalling and fearful at the time. But if one accepts it as Providence and surrenders to the process, one finds the emerging of the deep Self. One looks back on the event, and sees that at such a time there seems to be a spiritual power entering, a kind of enlightenment and healing . . . It takes different forms for different people, but underneath the seeming tragedy, there is always the spirit of Love operating in and through it all for the good of the individual.

Aware of the numbers of caregivers and staff members who were accompanying some of the patients at his talk and out of genuine compassion for each person there, he made a final closing statement:

> Finally I want to say that I have found unselfish love to be one of the keys. If anyone is giving their life in unselfish love, it can open up this deep centre, this deep Self, and spiritual power enters one's life. It is in everyone. This is the great journey of meditation: to surrender the ego, the ordinary personal consciousness with all its programs, fears and automatic reactions to the circumstances of life, and open in love to the deep Self, the transcendent. It is Love that will lead to happiness and peace. This is my prayer for you all today.

Father Bede's daily walk to and from celebrating the Eucharist,
Saccidananda ashram

# Postscript

I believe that Western Australia and, in fact, the whole nation has benefited tremendously from Father Bede Griffiths' two visits of 1985 and 1992. Though he was a man of incisive intellect and regarded by some as one of the most influential spiritual teachers of the last century, he was a humble man of great simplicity and goodness. I am privileged to have known and lived with him. As with Bede, my life has had its share of sudden breakthroughs; and while some of them have tested me to the limit, all have in some mysterious way been part of the unfolding of Love in my life. Many clergy give assent to the notion of interfaith dialogue, though I suspect not too many would be comfortable with walking the extra mile – trekking the Himalayas and seeking out teachers of Buddhist and Hindu meditation. My activities in interfaith dialogue have not always endeared me to some in the church. Some years ago, at a time of modest new potential for achievement within my profession, suddenly my work, and for a while peace of mind, was swept away by events beyond my control. In spite of the darkness that overwhelmed me, I hung on to the abiding sense that God and the universe were 'not two,' but one transcendent whole, and that it is ultimately benevolent. In spite of and within the pain and woundedness of life, for millions who suffer sudden illness, the collapse of a career, or betrayal for instance, there may be a recognition: it is that Love embraces all. Herein lies hope of peace and happiness. Without the inspiration of Bede Griffiths' vision of reality and belief in the transcendent One beyond all name and forms, I doubt I would have had the inner resources to come through that period and write this book.

In the final two weeks of Father Bede's Australian tour of 1992, I returned to pastoral duties in Western Australia, and he continued on to Brisbane. Bede was by now very weak, and I wondered if he should continue travelling. He insisted, asserting gently: "I must do what I can to spread the word for as long as God gives me strength." While preparing to say goodbye, Bede thanked me, saying: "You took care of me in every way possible. You didn't let me take a single step without making sure it was safe for me. I felt very cared for. I shan't forget this period with you and our many friends in this country."

It is my hope that in these stories my readers will also sense the wonder of the man who was, as his biographer Shirley du Boulay wrote: ". . . like yeast, leavening the flour and water of institutional religion, seeing its point of transcendence where all is one and all is love."

# Glossary:

*advaita*, non-duality, not-two

*ashram*, monastery, 'abode of the ascetics'; also *asrama* — stage of life.

*atman*, the Self, a person's innermost principle, the soul considered in its inmost essence independent of its mental or sensory faculties

*brahmacharya*, a celibate student; one in the first *asrama* (first of the four stages of life) at a deeper level, it means a 'vow of holiness,' 'moving in Brahman,' 'dwelling in God' — 'his thoughts are thinking on me'

*brahman*, the supreme principle of all; the creative source of all that is; the sacred principle and mystery lying behind all things; the Absolute

*Dzogchen*, (meditation) — *dzog* means 'perfection,' *chen*, means 'great.' Developed in the tenth and eleventh centuries in the Chinese Ch'an Tradition and integrated into Tibet by Padmasambhava; it is a way of experiencing the fullness of wisdom and compassion.

*guru*, lit. "heavy, weighty", gravity, grace, etc. . . . hence elder, venerable, (also Sanskrit root for Lama — 'heavy with teaching'), one who not only knows, but is able to pass on and teach his/her experience and knowledge. Such a one is (1) well versed in sacred scriptures — *srotriya*, having 'heard' much, and (2) fully established in the Absolute Reality - *brahmanistha*.

*saccidananda*, Being (*sat*) Knowledge (*cit*) Bliss (*ananda*)

*sannyasi, samnyasi*, one who has renounced everything, has given him/her self up to the cosmic life.

*Shantivanam*, Forest of Peace — the name of the place surrounding Saccidananda ashram

*siva maheswara*, The Great God Siva

*yoga*, Sanskrit root — *yuj*, to yoke together, to unite. The way of union. Various practices that attempt to bring about physical, mental and spiritual harmony and an ascent to Godhead.

# Acknowledgments to the Publishers:

The author acknowledges with gratitude the courtesy of those publishers, other organisations and individuals who have given special permission to use extracts from their copyright material, and thanks are also due to others whose copyright material has been included in this book. Thank you to the following for their permissions.

# Select Bibliography

## Books by Bede Griffiths
*The Cosmic Revelation: The Hindu Way to God*, Springfield, Illinois: Templegate Publishers, 1983.
*The Golden String: An Autobiography*, Springfield, Illinois: Templegate Publishers, 1954, 1980.
*The Marriage of East and West: A Sequel to The Golden String*, Springfield, Illinois: Templegate Publishers, 1982.
*The New Creation in Christ: Christian Meditation and Community*, Springfield, Illinois: Templegate Publishers, 1994.
*A New Vision of Reality: Western Science, Eastern Mysticism and Christian Faith*, Springfield, Illinois: Templegate Publishers, 1990.
*Return to the Centre*, Springfield, Illinois: Templegate Publishers, 1977.

*River of Compassion: A Christian Commentary on the Bhagavad Gita*, Springfield, Illinois: Templegate Publishers, 2001.
*Vedanta and Christian Faith*, Los Angeles, California: The Dawn Horse Press, 1973.

## Books by Authors about Bede Griffiths

Conlan, Meath. "Journey to the Cave of the Heart: Spiritual Direction and the Unfolding of the Self at Mid-life". MA Dissertation. Fordham University, New York, 1996.

———. "Love is the Golden String". *The Tablet*. (2 June 2001): pp. 795-796.

Du Boulay, Shirley. *Beyond the Darkness: A Biography of Bede Griffiths*. Rider, London, 1998.

## Other Sources

Abhishiktananda, Swami. *Saccidananda: A Christian Approach to Hindu Advaita.* Delhi: ISPCK, 1990.

Borges, Jose Luis. "Blindness." in *Seven Nights*, New Directions, New York. 1984.

Fox, Matthew. *The Re-invention of Work: A New Vision of Livelihood for our Time*. San Francisco: HarperSanFranscisco, 1994

Jones, Caroline. *The Search for Meaning*. Sydney: Australian Broadcasting Corporation, 1989.

Lawrence, D. H. in *Poems* (Revised Edition). p. 216. Selected and introduced by Keith Sagar. Penguin Poetry Library, PenguinBooks, Middlesex. UK, 1986.

Namkhai, Chogyal Norbu, 2000. *The Crystal and the Way of Light*, Snow Lion Publications. Ithaca, NY. www.SnowLionPub.com.

Rajan, Jesu. "Christian Interpretation of Indian Sannyasa." Doctoral Dissertation. Pontifical University of St. Thomas, Rome, 1988.

Stockton, Eugene. *Land Marks: A Spiritual Search in a Southern Land*. Eastwood, Australia: Parish Ministry Publications, 1990.

———. 'Sacred Story – Sacred Land,' *Compass Theology Review (1990)*, Vol. 25, 11-2 pp. 5-14.

# Index

Abhishiktananda, Swami (Fr Henri Le Saux) 56, 124
Afghan, community (Western Australia) 21
Africa 11, 72
Albany 18, 19, 20
Ama Samy, Fr 35, 36-39, 59, 127
Amaldas, Swami 44, 45, 112
Arico, Carl 14
Arjuna, Prince 65, 66-67
Armani, Gianni & Eleonora 13
Armani, Pietro 14
Australia 11-12, 15, 17, 20, 21-24, 27-30, 44, 72, 74, 79, 81, 85, 91-97, 99, 103, 111, 112, 125
Baker, Jack 14
Bott, David 14
Bott, family 13
Brahman 33, 35, 45, 54, 104, 121
Brennan, Bill & Christine 13
Brisbane 120
Buddha, Guatama 65, 88-89
Buddhism 41, 59, 68, 72, 84, 89, 103, 104, 107, 127
Bunning, Helen 14
Caproni, Maria Fede 14
Carey, Robert 13
Cauvery, River 34, 60
China, People's Republic of 87, 127
Christ 15, 27, 33, 43, 53, 89
Christian 40, 41, 53, 56, 62, 68, 84, 87, 88 89, 90, 91, 96, 103, 104, 105, 107, 109, 111, 115, 127
Christudas, Fr 63, 79
Cistercian Monks 14
Clark, Manning 11
Clement of Alexandria, Saint 105
Coff, Sr Pascaline 13, 15-16, 34
Conlan, Doug (author's father) 5, 17, 19
Conlan, Meath 10, 14, 15-16, 21-24, 28-30, 33-40, 45-48, 124, 127-28
Conlan, Nancy 5, 14, 17, 19
Croker, Alan 13
Dalai Lama, the XIVth of Tibet 19, 71-72, 99-101, 104-9, 127
Daly River, Australia 93

Day, Anne 13
Desert Fathers and Mothers 24
Dhyananda, Swami (Fr Bede Griffiths) 9
Dindigal, Tamil Nadu 36-38
Dionysius, the Areopagite 104, 107, 108
Do Rosario, Loretta 13
Dostoevsky, Fyodor 31
Douglas, John 13
Du Boulay, Shirley 120, 124
Duffy, Dan & Del 14
Dwyer, Fr Barry 13
Dzogchen 84, 86-89, 100, 121
Edleman, Dianne 14
Elephanta caves, India 73
Elliott, Herb 13
Fitzgerald River National Park 22, 28
Francis de Sales, Saint 89
Francis of Assisi, Saint 44
Freeman, Fr Laurence 13
Gaboo, Elder 92, 93, 95, 96, 97, 98
Gagnon, Jerry 14
Ganesh, Lord 46
Garvey, Thomas 12-13
Gates, Bruce 14
Gawler, Dr Ian 111-12
Ghandi, Mahatma 22
Gnowangerup, Western Australia 22
Goenka, Sri S.N. 36
Good Samaritan Sisters 14
Great Victoria Desert 21
Griffiths, Father Bede 2, 9-12, 14, 15-16, 17-20, 21-24, 27-28, 30-31, 33-36, 38, 40-41, 43-45, 46-51, 53-54, 56, 58, 59-64, 65-69, 71-77, 79-84, 85-90, 91-98, 99-101, 103-9, 111-17, 119-20, 123-24, 127-28
Halsall, Joan 14
Heerman, Barry & Kipra 14
Hinduism 41, 63, 65, 68, 72, 103, 104, 107
Hohnen, Mark & Cate 13
Holland, Ken 14
Howie, Andrew 13
India 9-10, 20, 22-24, 30, 33, 38, 40, 43, 53, 54, 57, 59, 62, 65, 71, 72-74, 80, 113, 125, 126, 128

Ishpriya Mataji 53-54, 127
Jesus 56- 84, 90
John Paul II, Pope 44
Jones, Caroline 11-12, 124
Jordhen, Ven Lobsang 100
Kain, Dr Anthony 13
Kauravas, the Kingdom of 66
Keating, Thomas 14
Ketudat, Emilie & Sipphanonda 13
Khejok, Tulku Rinpoche 13, 128
Kingsley, George & Anthea 14
Krishna, Lord 19, 67
Kurisamala ashram, Kerala 9
Lao Tzu 65
Lassalles, Fr Hugo Enomiya 35, 36-38, 59
Lautner, John & Helen 14
Lawrence, D.H. 48-49, 58, 124
Le Saux, Fr Henri (Swami Abhishiktananda) 56
Loden, Ven Geshse Thubten 86-87, 90
Manjusri, sword of 38
Marist Fathers 14
Martin, Br John 13
McAlinden, Kieran 14
McPherson, Jann 14
Melbourne, Australia 14, 85, 86, 87, 111
Mifsud, Fr. Michael 13
Monchanin, Fr Jules (Swami Paramarubyananda) 56, 96
Moore, Thomas 12
Moslem 21, 41
Nagarjuna 107
Nagasaki, Japan 37
Nehru, Jawaharlal 34
New South Wales 92, 93, 98
Newton, Sir Isaac 48
Ngangikurungkurr, Tribe of indigenous Australians 93
Nicholl, Donald 74-75
Norbu, Ven Namkhai 82, 87, 124
Padmasambhava 121
Pandavas, the Kingdom of 66
Partridge, Nicholas 13
Paul, Saint 91
Perrott, Michael & Rhonda 14
Perth 13, 14, 19, 21, 79, 99, 105
Pignedoli, Sergio Cardinal 127
Porter, Cherie & Dan 14
Rahner, Karl 89
Rajan, Fr Jesu 54, 124
Red Army 87

Reid, Kerrie 13
Rimmington, Richard & Jacinta 14
Roach, David 13
Romans, Saint Paul's Letter to the 91
Romuald, Saint 69
Ropers, Roland & Christiane 14
Saccidananda ashram, ashram of the Holy Trinity 24, 33, 40, 46, 50, 53, 56, 60, 80, 90, 114, 117, 122, 124, 127
Saint John of God, Sisters of 14
Saint Joseph, Sisters of 14, 79
Schwab, Phil & Mary 14
Shankara, Acharya 106
Shantivanam, 'Forest of Peace' 12, 15, 34 35, 38, 40, 49, 51, 55, 56, 57, 59, 62, 68, 80, 90, 111, 112, 122
Sheehan, Canon Frank 13
Singapore 45
Siva, Maheswara 73, 122
Skipper, Stephen & Mandy 14
Soviet Union 43
Spearritt, Placid 14
Stockton, Fr Eugene 94, 95, 124
Sumich, John 13-14
Sydney 13, 14, 93
Taoism 33, 72, 103, 104
Taubner, Val & Joan 14
Teasdale, Dr Wayne 34
Terry, Paul & Joan 18, 19
Tethong, Tenzin Geshe 100, 104, 105
Thomas Aquinas, Saint 106
Tibet 34, 40, 87, 99, 100, 108-9, 121, 128
Trapnell, Dr Judson 40-41
Ungunmerr, Miriam-Rose 93
Vajra Verses, the Six 79, 82-84, 87
Vandana Mataji 53-54, 127
Wallaga Lake, indigenous People 92, 93
Walsh, Barry and Jan 13
Walsh, Dr Michael Adrian 5, 13
Walsh, John T. 14
Western Australia 19-20, 21-22, 53, 59, 71, 82, 99, 105, 119-20
Wilkins, John 13
Williams, Professor Colin 11
Willis, Dr Peter 13
Wordsworth, William 80-81

# About the Author

Australian Meath Conlan, Ph.D., author and spiritual counsellor in private practice, has travelled extensively through the world of spiritual traditions. He undertook his first Buddhist *vipassana* meditation training in Thailand at the age of eighteen. 'Inter-spirituality', dialogue between religions, and contemplative renewal have long been sources of interest for him. On a number of official delegations from 1977 to 1982 he represented his friend, the late Sergio Cardinal Pignedoli, Prefect of the then Secretariat for Non-Christian Religions, in the People's Republic of China. The purpose of this mission was to build bridges of understanding between Christians and members of other religions in China.

Ordained a Roman Catholic priest in 1973, and serving a number of remote rural parishes for many years, he took his sabbatical (1984) with Bede Griffiths at *Saccidananda ashram* in South India. Since then, with Bede's mentoring, he has been active in interfaith dialogue between Christians, Buddhists, Moslems, and Hindus. Dr Conlan leads small groups on pilgrimage to the holy places of these religions.

During their speaking tours from 1985 through 1992 Meath Conlan hosted Bede Griffiths, Zen Master Ama Samy, Vandana Mataji and Ishpriya in Australia. At the request of His Holiness the XIVth Dalai Lama, Dr Conlan has lectured on the Western contemplative tradition to Tibetan Buddhist monastics in the Himalayas since 1989. As a further contribution to inter-religious dialogue, he has also travelled in Tibet, Nepal and India with his friend, Tibetan teacher Khejok Tulku Rinpoche over a period of years. He is an honorary member of Dhe Tsang Buddhist Monastery community in Eastern Tibet.

Upon Father Bede's death in May 1993, Dr Conlan was appointed to The Bede Griffiths Trust (www.bedegriffiths.com). He holds a Master of Arts Degree in Religion from Fordham University in New York, and Doctor of Philosophy from the University of South Australia. To find out more about his written works, retreats and spiritual journeys in Asia and elsewhere, please go to his personal website: www.diversejourneys.net or contact him directly by email: DrConlan@diversejourneys.net